REVISITING VICTIMS' PARTICIPATION AT THE ICC: Advocacy for an Efficient Restorative International Criminal Justice System

GRACIEUX MBUZUKONGIRA

REVISITING VICTIMS' PARTICIPATION AT THE ICC: Advocacy for an Efficient Restorative International Criminal Justice System

GALDA VERLAG 2020

Bibliografische Information der Deutschen Nationalbibliothek
Die Deutsche Nationalbibliothek verzeichnet diese Publikation in der Deutschen Nationalbibliografie; detaillierte bibliografische Daten sind im Internet über http://dnb.ddb.de abrufbar.

ISBN 978-3-96203-133-6 (Print)
ISBN 987-3-96203-134-3 (Ebook)

Justice only justice shall thou pursue…
A King shall through the exercise of justice establish a land,
but one that loveth gifts overthroweth it.
THE TALMUD

CONTENTS

ABSTRACT

This research submits that for the purposes of making victims' participation to the ICC proceedings more efficient, the victims' status could be raised to a status similar to that of *partie civile* common in civil law jurisdictions. However such status should be limited to victims who are ready to take the solemn oath and who accept to be cross-examined and who understand that should they give false evidence to the Court, they would become subject to criminal proceedings for attempt to subvert the Court's administration of justice. Furthermore the Chamber should have the discretion to grant such status to any victim it deems fit according to the relevance of submissions they intend to make.

It further submits that whereas criminal proceedings should remain the focus of their primary mission which is establishing guilt, the reparation mechanism should be victim centered. Indeed one may be tempted to advocate for a reparation system which is less judicial even when such mechanism might remain within the ICC auspices; the mechanism should rather be more restorative, thus leaning more towards mechanisms available under transitional justice.

The annex to this book is made of a list of some legal texts selected from the Rome Statute and the Rules of Procedure and Evidence reflecting the consideration given to the concept of victim by the ICC

ACKNOWLEDGEMENTS

This research has been conducted mainly at the Max-Planck-Institute for Comparative Public and International Law in Heidelberg, I take this opportunity to thank the Directors of the Institute, Professor Armin von Bogdandy and Professor Anne Peters for having opened the doors of the Institute for me once again and allowing me to carry out this research at the Institute.

In a special way I want to thank His Excellency Ambassador Mohammed Sani and Professor Mathias Sahinkuye of the African Institute of International Law in Arusha for having welcomed me at their Institute and having allowed me access at their various resources as well.

During this research I benefited from other scholars' contributions, in particular Dr. iur. Peter Smith Maccalister and Professor Roland Adjovi of Arcadia University for the discussion we had at the beginning of this project, I am forever grateful for the exchange we had.

I thank Colin Flinn for having accepted to proofread my draft and correct my grammar mistakes however any shortcomings shall remain exclusively mine.

I wish to express my gratitude to Mr Hillary Kimeu of the Catholic University of Eastern Africa for his exemplary dedication for his work. Such a commitment has been inspirational to me.

I could not have carried out this research without the financial assistance I received from two German institutions namely the *Max-Planck Gesellschaft* and the *Deutcher Akademischer Austauschdienst*. However, I wish to acknowledge the *Max-Planck Gesellshaft* in a special way.

I thank my family for having been supportive. Kristina Kwite, Maria Batete, McNgabo and Loic Hakiza, the gang that surrounds me all seasons.

This book is humbly dedicated to Lydia MaheKay.
She knows why.

1

INTRODUCTION

According to Judge Van den Wyngaert, victim's participation is one of the factors that led scholars and practitioners to conclude that the ICC was shifting the international criminal justice system from a retributive to a restorative justice system.[1]

However, considering that the Rome Statute did not abandon its retributive purpose rather than attempt to incorporate some elements of restorative justice, namely victim's participation and reparation by compensating either individually or collectively with the aim reinstating victims in their dignity, the ICC could thus be said to combine a retributive justice with a restorative mission.[2]

Such combination can be seen from the preamble of the Rome Statute which highlights that "during this century millions of children, women and men have been victims of unimaginable atrocities that deeply shock the conscience of humanity"[3] and also recognising that "such grave crimes threaten the peace, security and well-being of the world"[4] hence the determination "to put an end to impunity for the perpetrators of these crimes and thus to contribute to the prevention of such crimes."[5]

This chapter intends to discuss concepts of victims and restorative justice by tracing them from their early practice to contemporary practices before proceeding to a brief overview of the current literature on the subject.

---

[1]Christine Van den Wyngaert.2011. Victims before International Criminal Courts: Some Views and Concerns of an ICC Trial Judge. *44 Case W. Res. J. Int'l L. 475*. p 476

[2]Kelisiana Thynne.2009. The International Criminal Court: A Failure of International Justice for Victims. *46 Alta. L. Rev. 957*. p 963

[3]See the Preamble of the Rome Statute para 2

[4]Idem, Para 3

[5]T. Markus Funk.2015. Surveying the Rise of Victims' Rights under International Law (and at the International Criminal Court). *11 Eyes on the ICC 3*. p 7

1. The Concept of Restorative Justice

Whereas retributive justice focuses on punishment as decided by criminal justice system, restorative justice sees a crime as a conflict between individuals. It considers that the injuries inflict a crime on all parties including the victim, the perpetrator and the society as whole.[6]

Hence it focuses on the victims of the crime, acknowledges their suffering and attempts to restore the damage[7] by reinstating the victim's sense of dignity amongst other things by their participation to the process.[8]

2. Early Victims' Centered Justice

As said by Weitekamp, victim-centered justice might have existed since humans began forming communities.[9] For instance, it is recorded that such a justice system is found in the famous Code of Hammurabi (1750 BC).[10] Indeed, §22. The Hammurabi's Code of Laws, provided that: "If any one is committing a robbery and is caught, then he shall be put to death."[11]

However §23 of the same Code said: "If the robber is not caught, then he who was robbed shall claim under oath the amount of his loss; then shall the community, ... on whose ground and territory and in whose domain it was committed shall compensate him for the goods stolen."[12] Further, §55 of the same Code said that: "If any one open his ditches to water his crop, but is careless, and the water flood the field of his neighbour, then he shall pay his neighbour corn for his loss."[13]

---

[6]Karen Brounéus. Reconciliation and Development. *International Conference Building a Future on Peace and Justice.* Nuremberg, 25-27 June 2007. p7

[7]Jemima Garcia-Godos.2008. Victim Reparations in Transitional Justice, What is at Stake and Why. *26 Nordisk Tidsskrift for Menneskerettigheter 2.* p119

[8]Anuradha Saibaba Rajesh. 2009. Victims in the International Criminal Court: Vindicated or Vanquished. *9 ISIL Y.B. Int'l Human. & Refugee L. 120.* p 126

[9]Elmar G. M. Weitekamp. *The History of Restorative Justice* as cite by Douglas J. Sylvester. 2002. Myth in Restorative Justice History. *2003 Utah Law Review 1.* p 500

[10]Ilaria Bottigliero.2004. *Redress for Victims of Crimes under International Law.* Martinus Nijhoff Publishers. p 15.

[11]See § 22 of the Hammurabi's Code of Laws

[12]See § 23 of the Hammurabi's Code of Laws

[13]See § 55 of the Hammurabi's Code of Laws

Thus, the compensation driven system of justice which is inspired by the principle of "*restitution en nature*" could be also termed as restorative justice. It is a philosophy that focuses more on reparation of the damage caused by a crime.[14] Such philosophy could find in the spirit of The Laws of Manu which could be dated ca. 200 BC.[15]

According to §40 of Chapter VIII of The Laws of Manu "Property stolen by thieves must be restored by the king to (men of) all caste (varna)..."[16] the same chapter of the same code in its §241 provides that: "(For damage) in other fields (each head of) cattle shall (pay a fine of one (pana) and a quarter, and in all (cases the value of) the crop (destroyed) shall be made good to the owner of the field; that is the settled rule."[17]

Perhaps the oldest record of this philosophy can be found in ancient Egypt. The Egyptian legal system predicated on the Ma'at, the Goddess of Justice, required the judge to create a remedy where there was a gap in the written law or where the strict application of law would yield a harsh result.[18]

However, over time the restorative system of justice seems to have lost its popularity to retributive justice, which rather focuses more on the punishment that must be administered to the offender, leaving aside the victim and the reparation system.

Indeed, already in 1646 the philosopher Grotiuos Hugo, was suggesting that: "Vengeance, even if it is exacted by a private individual, is not unlawful

---

[14]Jim Consedine. 1999. The Third Millennium - Restorative Justice or more Crime and Prisons? *Sri Lanka Journal of International Law 11*. p 2

[15]The Law of Manu is the most important and earliest metrical work of the Dharmaśāstra textual tradition of Hinduism which was composed of 2685 decrees and prohibition in the ancient Hindu see http://www.duhaime.org/LawMuseum/LawArticle-297/200-BC--Laws-of-Manu.aspx, their precise date is unknown it is however suggested that they might have been established in India by the 5th Century and possibly as early as the 3rd century. See Patric Olivelle. 2005. *Manu's Code of Law, A Critical Edition and Translation of the Manava-Dharmásatra*. Oxford University Press. p 3

[16]See §40 of Chapter VIII of The Laws of Manu

[17]Id. §241, The Patric Olivelle tarnsaltion says: "When damage is done [...] in every case, the owner of the field ought to be compensated for the crop- That is the fixed rule." See Patric Olivelle. 2005. *Manu's Code of Law, A Critical Edition and Translation of the Manava-Dharmásatra*. Oxford University Press. p 180.

[18]Frankfort, et al.1951. *Before Phylosophy*, Pelican. pp 99-100, as cited by R. Neil Snyder. *Natural Law and Equity*, in Ralph A. Newman.1973. *Equity in the world's legal systems, a comparative study*, Etablissements Emile Bruylant. p 35

according to the bare law of nature."[19] Nevertheless time eroded such a philosophy, as a given crime became considered as an offence first against the existing order, consequently against the King and deserved to be punished accordingly. Hence, for the purposes of restoring the violated order, such crime deserved punishment by "reasserting in emphatic terms the outraged authority."[20] This move prompted the replacement of restorative justice by the retributive justice approach as it strongly affected the role played by victims.

Indeed, retributive justice seems not to address the victim's concerns. Therefore, as said by Rishi:

> Ancient societies recognised the natural right of a victim to inflict punishment on the wrongdoer by way of revenge. With the passage of time, it was realised that the victim should not be allowed to take the law into his own hands for these purposes. Instead of that, the State or the society should consider it to be its collective duty to ensure the criminal or the wrongdoer got suitably punished. While this principle became universal, the victim started getting ignored altogether.[21]

Obviously, the role played by victims in justice declined as the restorative system of justice became progressively replaced by a retributive justice approach.[22] Retributive theories of punishment maintain that criminal merits or deserves punishment, regardless of consideration of its social utility.[23]

However, such a view became associated with the necessary consideration of the utility of punishment. The utilitarianism of a punishment could be found

---

[19]Hugo Grotious.1995. *De Jure Belli ac Pacis Libri Tres*. Translation Book I by Francis W. Kelsey, William S. Hein. p 472

[20]Sheldon Amos. 1881. *The Science of law, Fifth Edition*, C. Kegan Paul & CO.

[21]D.D. Rishi. 1998. Victim and Punishment of the Offender. In *Human Rights and Victimology*. cited by Timothy K. Kuhner. p 106

[22]D.D. Rishi. 1998. Victim and Punishment of the Offender. In *Human Rights and Victimology*. cited by Timothy K. Kuhner. p 106

[23]Jeffrie G. Murhpy. 1979. *Retribution Justice and Therapy, Essays in the Philosophy of Law*. Reidel Publishing Company. p 77 for further reference See Jeffrie G. Murphy. 1992. *Retribution Reconsidered: More essays in the philosophy of Law*, Kluwer Academic Publishers. p 21 saying: "Retributivists seeks, not primarily for the socially useful punishment, but for the just punishment, the punishment that the criminal deserves or merits."

in Jeremy Bentham's [1748-1832][24] writings saying: "There are accordingly three courses which the law may take in obviating the mischief: to make compensation for what is past, to cure, that is to put a stop, what is present, and to guard against what might otherwise be to come."[25]

Whereas John Austin's [1790-1859] theory of utility of punishment is found in his writing saying that "though considered in isolation, a punishment might be an evil, the pain inflicted on the criminal being added to the mischief of the crime. But considered as part of a system, a punishment is useful or beneficent."[26] The same philosopher goes on explaining that: "By a dozen or score of punishment, thousands of crimes are prevented. With sufferings of the guilty few, security of the many is purchased. By the lopping of a peccant member, the body is saved from decay."[27]

3. Reconciliation of Retributive and Restorative Justice

Because justice became more retributive, victims lost their place in the course of the process. A thorough analysis of theory of utilitarianism punishment could lead to the conclusion that punishing the criminal does not necessarily have to exclude providing remedy to the victims.

Furthermore, restoring the victims' dignity might be restored in a punitive way from the offender's perspective, as "[t]he punisher who inflicts retribution on such a wrongdoer wants to reassert those facts and vindicate the value of the victim."[28] As said by Susan Dimock: "The criminal denies the equal value of their victims, and this false value claim must be annulled or rebutted by punishment. By punishing criminals we subject them to a defeat, and we thereby demonstrate that their claimed superiority is false,"[29]therefore deterring potential criminals from their desire to commit crimes.

[24]Edgar Bodenheimer.1962. *Jurisprudence: The philosophy and Method of the Law.* Harvard University Press. p 82

[25]Jeremy Bentham. 1945. *The Limits of Jurisprudence Defined*, Columbia University Press. p 240

[26]Robert Campbell. 1885. *Lectures on Jurisprudence or the Philosophy of Positive Law by the Late John Austin.* Fifth Edition. John Murray. p 108

[27]Id.,

[28]Jean Hampton. 1991. An Expressive Theory of Retribution. In *Retrbutivism and its Critics.* Franz Steiner Veröags Stuttgart. p12

[29]Susan Dimock. 1963. *Classic Readings and Cases in the Philosophy of Law.* Pearson Longman. p 559

Such a tendency re-activates the role plaid by victims without excluding the punishment of the offender, as both type of justice were understood as complementing without excluding each other. However the point of view that combines the utilitarian aspect of a punishment contained in its deterrent role and its retributive aspect has been subject of debate between consequentialists and deontologists.[30]

One may argue that apparently contrary principles of retribution and reparation can be viewed as dependent on one another. Indeed, both censure and reparation need to occur before a victim or community can reintegrate an offender into the community.[31] Thus the view that restorative and distributive justice are incompatible might be partially mistaken.[32] Restorative justice should not be viewed in opposition to retributive. Instead, retributive justice needs to be coupled with restorative justice to achieve its purposes.

It is in that line that in 1928 the Permanent Court of International Justice held that the right to reparation is an indispensable complement and that reparation must re-establish the situation which would have existed if the act had not been committed.[33] It is important to note that both restorative and retributive justice acknowledge that moral equilibrium is regained only when the victim's dignity is acknowledged, the offender held accountable, and the community's moral norm re-affirmed.[34]

The ICC lay in its potential to deter war criminal and crimes against humanity by providing a balanced instrument of both retributive and restorative justice. It is this attempt to reach a balance between punishment of those who commit crimes and justice for victims of those crimes which gives the ICC purposes.

---

[30]For further information on the debate, see Mark R. Reiff. 2005. Punishment, Compensation and Law: A Theory of Enforceability. Cambridge University Press. p 124

[31]Kathleen Daly. 2004. Restorative Justice: The Real Story. In *Restorative Justice*. Ashgate Dartmouth. p 90

[32]Charles Barton. 2000. Empowerment and Retribution in Criminal Justice. In *Restorative Justice, Philosophy to Practice*, Ashgate. pp 55-56

[33]Chorzow Factory (Indemnity). PCIJ (Ser A.) No 17. p 29, 47 as cited by Michael G. Palmer.2004. Compensation for Vietnam's Agent Orange Victims, in *8 International Journal of Human Rights 1*. p 4.

[34]Ellen A. Waldman. 2003. Healing Hearts or Righting Wrongs?: A Meditation on the Goals of Restorative Justice, in *25 Hamline Journal of Public Law & Policy 1*. p 356

The Rome Statute created a framework, which took forward the development of the 1990s into the 21st century.[35] Indeed, as said by Silvia D'Ascoli:

> In the 1980, one of the major developments in criminal justice was the increasing recognition of the rights and needs of victims of crimes. It was affirmed that seeking justice and reparation for victims should be considered as one of the most relevant purposes pursued by a system of criminal justice.[36]

4. Victim- Centered Justice through Truth and Reconciliation

The truth and reconciliation process is understood as a type of transitional justice that a country would resort to as a response to a past crisis that the classic justice system might not be able to cope with for the purposes of restoring national reconciliation.[37] As said by Alvarez, the constitution of truth and reconciliation has a double objective including "to preserve collective memory[[38]] and appease the victim."[39]

Victims play a key role in the process[40] of which they are considered masters. Indeed, the truth and reconciliation process is a victim centered[41] justice achieved through of restorative justice. Though no standard definition of restorative justice exists, it is considered as a healing process that involves

---

[35]Vasselin Popovski.2000. The international Criminal Court: A Synthesis of Retributive and Restorative Justice, in *XV International Relations 3.* p 9

[36]Silvia D'Ascoli. 2011. *Sentencing in International Criminal Law, the UN Ad Hoc Tribunals and Future Perspectives for the ICC*, Hart Publishing. p 70

[37]Paul Roberts and Nesam McMillan. 2003. For Criminology in International Justice. In *Journal of International Criminal Justice 1.* p 334

[38]Abdreas O' Shea. 2011. Truth and Reconciliation Commissions. In *Max-Planck Encyclopedia of Public International Law.* para. 1

[39]J.E. Alvarez. 1999. Crimes of State/Crimes of Hate: Lessons from Rwanda, in *Yale Journal of International Law*. p482

[40]Tony F. Marshall. 1999. *Restorative Justice: An overview.* A report by the Home Office Research Development and Statistics Directorate. p 9 saying "Restorative justice is centrally concerned with *restoration*: restoration of the victim,"

[41]Janine Natalya Clark. 2009. The Limits of Retributive Justice: Findings of an Empirical Study in Bosnia and Hercegovina. In *Journal of International Criminal Justice 7.* p 480

a wide range of human feeling, including pardon and reconciliation between the offender and the victim.[42]

Such process of healing[43] is possible through a mechanism that gives an opportunity to the offender to publicly confess their crimes[44] at the same time that it gives the victims an opportunity to be heard when telling their stories. It is through telling their story that both victim and the offender reconcile[45] as the victim become rehabilitated,[46] and their dignity becomes restored by the regret of the offender.

Nevertheless, despite its undisputable achievement, victim's pardon should, at least in an ideal case, come from the victim who as a matter of individual decision decides then to forgive the offender. When pardon is granted as matter of state policy, it could amount in a double victimisation phenomenon, which on top of the offence they suffered are equally obliged for forgive the offender.

5. The Concept of Victim within the ICC Legal Regime

Within the ICC legal regime, the participatory right of victims is provided for by Art. 68(3) of the ICC Statute. Though the concept of victim is defined by Rule 85 of the Rules of Procedure and Evidence, hereinafter "The Rules," as meaning any "natural persons who have suffered harm as a result of the commission of any crime within the jurisdiction of the Court."[47]

---

[42]See for instance Michelle Maiese, saying that „Restorative justice is concerned with healing victims' wounds restoring offenders to law-abiding lives, and repairing harm done to interpersonal relationship and the community." Michelle Maiese, The aims of restorative justice, available at http://www.beyondintractability.org/essay/restorative_justice/

[43]Lyn S. Graybill rather speaks of "testimony as a therapeutic technique to restore the victim" Lyn S. Graybill. 2002. *Truth & Reconciliation in South Africa, Miracle or Model?* Lynne Rienner Publishers.

[44]Tzvetan Todorov.2009. Memory as Remedy for Evil. In *Journal of International Criminal Justice 7*. p 457

45Alexander L. Boraine. 2006. Transitional Justice: A Holistic Interpretation, *60 Journal of International Affaire1*. p21

[46]Kader Asmal. 2000. Truth Reconciliation and Justice: the South African Experience in Perspective. *63 The Modern Law Review 1*. p 1

[47]Though paragraph b of the same Rule 85 adds that organization and institutions can also be considered victims under the circumstances provided for by the same Rule.

The Rules have defined the concept for the purposes of operating the above mentioned Art. 68 (3) of the ICC Statute according to which: "Where the personal interests of the victims are affected, the Court shall permit their views and concerns to be presented and considered at stages of the proceedings determined to be appropriate by the Court and in a manner which is not prejudicial to or inconsistent with the rights of the accused and a fair and impartial trial."

It is in that spirit that in its decision of 18th January 2008, the Trial Chamber I held that: "[D]uring the trial stage of a case the right of victims to participate is principally dependent on whether their personal interests are affected in accordance with Article 68(3) of the Statute, and Rule 85 of the Rules which provides a definition of "victims" should be read in light of that Article."[48]

Nevertheless, the right to participate to the ICC proceedings which is rightfully considered the ICC's novel feature,[49] has proved to be the most controversial issue within the ICC legal framework thus far.

---

[48]See ICC, Situation in the Democratic Republic of the Congo, in the case of the Prosecutor v. Thomas Lubanga Dyilo, Trial Chamber I, Decision on victims' participation, No.: ICC-01/04-01/06, of 18 January 2008, para 93

[49]Though Professor William Schabas has traced the development of the rights of victim in contemporary international law, demonstrating that the concept is not new in international law. See William A. Schabas. 2007. *An Introduction to the International Criminal Court*. Third Edition. Cambridge University Press. pp325-326. The same having been argued by Carla Ferstman saying that: "The right to reparation for victims of international crimes is a well established though often unimplemented principle of international law that has been expressly guaranteed by global and regional instruments, and has been the subject of numerous declarations, resolutions and treaty texts" the same author summarizes international instrument providing for the right of victims for instance: Art. 8 of the 1948 Universal Declaration of Human Rights; Art. 2(3) of the 1966 International Covenant on Civil and Political Rights; Art. 6 of the 1965 International Convention on the Elimination of All Forms of Racial Discrimination; Art. 14 of the 1984 Convention against Torture and Other Cruel, Inhuman or Degrading Treatment or Punishment; Art. 39 of the 1989 Convention on the Rights of the Child; Art. 7 of the 1981 African Charter on Human and Peoples' Rights; Art. 25 of the 1969 American Convention on Human Rights; and Art. 13 of the 1950 European Convention for the Protection of Human Rights and Fundamental Freedoms. See also the 1985 Declaration of Basic Principles of Justice for Victims of Crime and Abuse of Power, UN General Assembly Res. A/RES/40/34, Annex, 40 UN GAOR Supp. (No. 53), UN Doc. A/40/53 (29 November 1985), at 214; and the Basic Principles and Guidelines on the Right to a Remedy and Reparation for Victims of Violations of International Human Rights and Humanitarian Law, UN Doc. E/CN.4/2000/62 (18 January 2000). See the 1983 European Convention on the Compensation of Victims of Violent Crime; and Council of Europe Recommendations No. R(85) 11 (1985) and No. R(87) 21 (1987). See Carla Ferstman. 2002. The Reparation Regime of the International Criminal Court: Practical Consideration. In *Leiden Journal of International Law*. pp-667-680

Indeed, within the ICC legal regime, the modality of participation of victims before the Court varies according to the nature of their intervention and to the stage of the proceedings. Such intervention could start from communications informing the prosecutor on crimes within the jurisdiction of the Court,[50] up to participation at trial[51] and eventually to the claim for reparation.[52]

At the investigation phase, Art. 15 of the Statute authorises the Prosecutor to receive written or oral testimony at the seat of the Court. Such participation could be granted to any individual or organisation in possession of any relevant information without necessarily being a victim of a crime.[53]

Thus, at the investigation phase, there is no need to establish the nexus between a crime and the harm suffered by a victim, as no link is required between participation and personal interest in a particular case or situation.[54]

At the trial stage however, for victims to stand in their own capacity and participate to the proceedings as such, they should meet the requirements of Article 68(3), that is, (i) they should have sought to participate individually as victims in the situation phase of the proceedings (ii)they should have personal interests that are affected by the case(iii) their participation must be appropriate and lastly (iv) the manner of participation must not be prejudicial to or inconsistent with the rights of the accused and a fair impartial trial.[55]

---

[50]Art. 15 of the Statute

[51]Judgment on the Appeals of The Prosecutor and The Defence against Trial Chamber I's Decision on Victims' Participation of 18 January 2008 para 109 in which the Appeals Chamber confirmed the finding of the Trial Chamber that "victims participating in the trial proceedings may, in principle, lead evidence pertaining to the guilt or innocence of the accused and challenge the admissibility or relevance of the evidence." However the judgment was not unanimous as partially dissenting Judge G.M. Pikis opposed the judgment on the same issue.

[52]Art. 75 of the Statute

[53]Art. 15 of the Statute says that the Prosecutor "may seek additional information from States, organs of the United Nations, intergovernmental or non-governmental organizations, or other reliable sources that he or she deems appropriate." Thus, the Statute does not limit participation to victim of crime during investigation.

[54]Situation in the Democratic Republic of the Congo, The Appeals Chamber, Judgment on victim participation in the investigation stage of the proceedings in the appeal of the OPCD against the decision of Pre-Trial Chamber I of 7 December 2007 and in the appeals of the OPCD and the Prosecutor against the decision of the Pre-Trial Chamber I of 24 December 2007, 19 December 2008, para 41

55Situation in the Democratic Republic of the Congo, The Appeals Chamber, Decision on victim participation in the appeal of the Office of Public Counsel for the Defense against Pre-Trial Chamber I's decision of 7 December 2007 and in the appeals of the Office of Public Counsel Defense against Pre-Trial Chamber I's decision of 24 December 2007, 30 June 2008, para 90

Much that there have been inconsistencies within the ICC jurisprudence, it could be read from the jurisprudence that that when read in combination with Art. 68 (3) the application of Rule 85 the victim needs to satisfy the following conditions: (i) the applicant must be a natural person (or a legal person as specified in the definition)[56] (ii) they must have suffered harm (iii) the crimes alleged by them must fall within the jurisdiction of the Court, and (iv) there must be a causal link between the crime and the harm suffered by the victim.[57]

In its applicability, it would mean that the jurisdictional requirement is met when the crime that caused the harm, is within the jurisdiction of the court in accordance with Art. 5 of the Statute which provides for the Court's jurisdiction *rationae materiae* over the crimes of genocide, crimes against humanity, war crimes and aggression, under the conditions defined by Art. 11 determining the jurisdiction of the Court *rationae temporis to* include crime committed after the entry into force of the Statute, and Art. 12 determining the Court jurisdiction *rationae loci* over crimes committed on the territory of any state party or by national of a State party.

This reasoning seems to be supported by the Trial Chamber I in the Thomas Lubanga case which found that:

> Rule 85 of the Rules does not have the effect of restricting the participation of victims to the crimes contained in the charges confirmed by Pre-Trial Chamber I, and this restriction is not provided for in the Rome Statute framework. Rule 85(a) of the Rules simply refers to the harm having resulted from the commission of a „crime within the jurisdiction of the Court" and to add the proposed additional element - that they must be the crimes alleged against the accused - therefore would be to introduce a limitation not found anywhere in the regulatory framework of the Court.[58]

[56]Robert Cryer et al. 2010. An Introduction to International Criminal Law and Procedure, Second Edition, Cambridge University Press. p 486

[57]Pre-Trial Chamber I Decision on the Applications for participation in the proceedings of a/0001/06, a/0002/06 and a/0003/06 in the case of the Prosecutor v. Thomas Lubanga Dyilo and of the investigation in the Democratic Republic of the Congo, of 31 July 2006, p 7. See as well Pre-Trial Chamber I Decision on the Applications for participation in the proceedings a/0004/06, to a/0009/06, a/0016/06, a/0063/06, a/0071/06, to a/0080/06 and a/0105/06 in the case of the Prosecutor v. Thomas Lubanga Dyilo of 20 October 2006, p 9. See Annalisa Ciampi, The international criminal court, in The law and Practice of International Courts and Tribunals, Vol. 5 No. 1, 2006, p 221

[58]Thomas Lubanga, Trial Chamber I, Decision on Victims' Participation 18.01.2008 para 93

However such an ideal interpretation is challenged by the huge number of victims, posing a logistical problem to the court and its limited resources.[59]

6. From the Rome Diplomatic Conference to the Rome Statute

In his opening speech Mr. Kofi Annan then Secretary-General of the United Nations already stressed that: „the overriding interest must be that of the victims and of the international community as a whole.“ [60]

Thus, Art. 68 of the Report of the Preparatory Committee on the Establishment of an International Criminal Court of UN Diplomatic Conference of Plenipotentiaries on the Establishment of an International Criminal Court provided that:

> 4. [The Court [shall] [may] permit the views and concerns of the victim to be presented and considered at appropriate stages of the proceedings where their personal interests are affected in a manner which is consistent with the rights of the accused and a fair and impartial trial.]
>
> [7. The rules of procedure shall include provisions giving effect to the United Nations Declaration of Basic Principles of Justice for Victims of Crime and Abuse of Power.]
>
> [8. Legal representatives of victims of crimes have the right to participate in the proceedings with a view to presenting additional evidence needed to establish the basis of criminal responsibility as a foundation for their right to pursue civil compensation.][61]

---

[59]The same has been argued by McLaughlin, see Colin T. McLaughlin. 2007. Victims and Witness Measures of the International Criminal Courts: A Comparative Analysis, in *The law and Practice of International Courts and Tribunals, A Practitioners' Journal*

[60]United Nations Diplomatic Conference of Plenipotentiaries on the Establishment of an International Criminal Court, Rome, 15 June - 1 7 July 1998 Official Records,Volume II, A/CONF.183/13 p 60 para 11

[61]United Nations Diplomatic Conference of Plenipotentiaries on the Establishment of an International Criminal Court, Rome, Italy 15 June-17 July 1998, A/CONF.183/2/Add.1, 14 April 1998

However, Canada submitted a proposal on the same according to which:

> 3. The Court shall permit the views and concerns of the victims to be presented and considered at stages of the proceedings determined to be appropriate by the Court where their personal interests are affected, in a manner which is not prejudicial to or inconsistent with the rights of the accused and a fair and impartial trial. Such views and concerns may be presented by legal representatives of the victims where the Court considers it appropriate, in accordance with the Rules of Procedure and Evidence.
>
> [6. In the exercise of its powers under this article, the Court shall take into consideration the United Nations Declaration of Basic Principles of Justice for Victims of Crime and Abuse of Power.]

Further, the Canadian proposal suggested two options according to which paragraph 6, could be included in the text, or to be included as a footnote.

In addition, Sierra Leone suggested that the Prosecutor be empowered to receive information from victims, intergovernmental and non-governmental organisations to trigger investigations and prosecutions, and that the Court must remain sensitive to the rights of victims.[62]

It should be noted that other than individual States, some organisations manifested particular interest to the rights of victims during the diplomatic conference. This is the case of the observer for the Victims' Rights Working Group who submitted that: „the establishment of an international criminal court was an important symbol for survivors of heinous crimes, but there would be no justice without justice for victims" as she further highlighted that there was increasing recognition of the need to take account of victims' rights as she advocated for provisions which will guarantee effective participation of victims in the proceedings.[63]

The same applies to the observer for the Women's Caucus for for Gender Justice in the International Criminal Court who was of the opinion that victims and non-governmental organisations should be allowed to present complaints prior to an investigation.[64]

---

[62]Idem, p 87 para 53

[63]Idem, p 90 paras 77-78

[64]Idem, p 96 para 74

Further Austria endorsed the statement of the European Union but specifically added that the tragedies in Rwanda and the former Yugoslavia had emphasized the need for an International Criminal Court, adding the procedural provisions must ensure the fair and effective operation of the Court, safeguard the rights of the accused and ease the procedure of giving evidence by victims.[65] Such submission seems to have been supported by Rwanda according to which victims should be authorised to appear before the court and be granted pecuniary reparation.[66]

It is noteworthy pointing out the Nepal position according to which interest of justice was to be served if victims could also be made parties to the trial.[67] Obviously such proposal met France's support which proposed that the Statute should include specific provisions on the access of victims to all stages of the proceedings and on their protection against reprisals in the light of shortcomings that had become apparent in the International Tribunals.[68]

As Malawi suggested that the Court should consider the fate of victims as one of its principal concerns,[69] Ireland stressed that for the Court to be truly effective, an enforcement mechanism for international humanitarian law must allow victims an audible and direct voice which did not depend upon a State party or the Security Council for its expression.[70]

7. The Concept of Victim and United Nations General Assembly

The UNGA concerns for victims and their rights for reparation is not a new phenomenon. Art. 8 of the UDHR manifests the intention of the UNGA to ensure that effective remedies are provided to victims whenever their rights have been infringed and they have harm.[71]

Thus, in its effort to assist Governments and the international community to secure justice and assistance for victims of crimes and victims of abuse of power, the UN General Assembly in 1985 adopted the Declaration of Basic

[65]Idem, p 85 paras 40 - 43
[66]Idem, p 104 para 113
[67]Idem, p 99 para 48
[68]Idem, p 101 para 74
[69]Idem, p 109 para 56
[70]Idem, p 200 para 106
[71]Art. 8 of the UDHR

Principles of Justice for Victims of Crime and Abuse of Power, which defined the a victim to mean a

> persons who, individually or collectively, have suffered harm, including physical or mental injury, emotional suffering, economic loss or substantial impairment of their fundamental rights, through acts or omissions that are in violation of criminal laws operative within Member States, including those laws proscribing criminal abuse of power.[72]

Further, the UN General Assembly was concerned about the right of victims of gross violations of international human rights law and serious violations of international humanitarian law to be honoured and to benefit from remedies and reparation in 2005 and adopted the Basic Principles and Guidelines on the Right to a Remedy and Reparation for Victims which defines the concept of victim as comprising:

> [P]ersons who individually or collectively suffered harm, including physical or mental injury, emotional suffering, economic loss or substantial impairment of their fundamental rights, through acts or omissions that constitute gross violations of international human rights law, or serious violations of international humanitarian law. Where appropriate, and in accordance with domestic law, the term "victim" also includes the immediate family or dependants of the direct victim and persons who have suffered harm in intervening to assist victims in distress or to prevent victimisation. [73]

It is nevertheless noteworthy asking why the discussions within the UNGA have thus far remained subject to soft law. Might this have been part of reasons that led to the conclusion that "despite the relevance of the subject, victims have insufficiently been considered by international norms?"[74]

---

[72]UNGA Resolution A/RES/40/34 Of 29 November 1985

[73]UNGA Basic Principles and Guidelines on the Right to a Remedy and Reparation for Victims of Gross Violations of International Human Rights Law and Serious Violations of International Humanitarian Law, Adopted and proclaimed by General Assembly resolution 60/147 of 16 December 2005, para. 8

[74]Fernandez de Casadevante Romani. 2010. International Law of Victims, *14 Max Planck Y.B. U.N. L. 219*. p 221

8. Research Question

This research intends to assess to what extent victim's participation to the ICC proceedings and its subsequent reparation mechanism has contributed to its restorative mission.

9. Research Methods

This research will take two approaches: a theoretical approach reflective of the actual creation of legal rules; and an implementation focused approach, reflecting on the observance and application of legal rules and the successes achieved in strengthening legality and for consolidating law.[75]

As defined by Banakar and Travers[76], the rule-based paradigm which consists of a study of a law with recourse to the exegesis authoritative argument that allows reading and criticising its content will be of great use for this research.

The study's focus will be doctrinal, analysing legal sources. It will be based on other sources, especially scholarly writings published in leading international and national periodicals, journals, newspapers, reports, Aide-Memoire, Travaux Preparatoires, reference works and other relevant data available.

10. Brief Survey of the Existing Literature

In her paper "Victim participation at the International Criminal Court: Achievements made and Challenges lying ahead," Mariana Pena has studied achievements made by the ICC as far as victims participation is concerned but also looked at various challenges that the Court has had so far.

For instance using the Thomas Lubanga case, she has challenged the assumption that interests of victims are taken care of by the Prosecution.[77] On

---

[75]Dzhangir Kerimov. 1989. *Methology of Law*. Progress Publishers. p 12

[76]Reza Banakar and Max Travers. 2005. *Law, Sociology and Method, Theory and Method in Socio-Legal Research*. Hart Publishing. p 8

[77]Mariana Pena. 2010. Victim Participation at the International Criminal Court: Achievements Made and Challenges Lying Ahead. In *16 ILSA Journal of International and Comparative Law*

a different note, referring to the Jean Pierre Bemba case, she has demonstrated how victims have been able to contribute to the controversial question of the local languages spoken in the Central Africa Republic,[78] hence her conclusion that "victims have contributed to a more comprehensive presentation of the cases, and have also assisted judges to have a better understanding of the context of the relevant case."[79]

As far as challenges are concerned, she addresses the question of large numbers of victims and related administrative and managerial difficulties by calling for a more effective administrative mechanism capable of handling large number of applicants.[80] She also advises the Registry to take a more proactive role during the processing phase by seeking the judges instruction on key issues and setting up a centralised response system."[81]

In the work titled "Victim Participation at the International Criminal Court and its Impact on Procedural Fairness," the author points out some inconsistencies within the ICC's jurisprudence as far as the interpretation of relevant provisions pertaining to victims' participation are concerned.[82] For instance, the test applied in assessing victims' participation to the ICC proceedings, which seems to have been the most controversial.

If one considers the Appeals Chamber's decision of 11 July 2008, reversing the decision of the Trial Chamber of 18 January on the ground that only victims of the situation or case before the Chamber, rather than victims of any crime within the jurisdiction of the Court could apply to participate to the proceedings.[83] However, on 19 December 2008, the Appeals Chamber overruled the decisions of 7th and 24th December 2007 of the PTC I which had granted victims participatory rights to the proceedings at the investigation phase.[84]

Bridie McAsey stresses how victims' participation under the ICC legal regime is rather left to various chambers to decide which position creates uncertainty considering inconsistencies within the jurisprudence. Maybe

---

2. p 502

[78]Idem

[79]Idem, p 503

[80]Idem, p 509

[81]Idem, p 512

[82]Bridie McAsey. 2011. Victim Participation at the International Criminal Court and its Impact on Procedural Fairness. In *Australian International Law Journal.* p 110

[83]Idem, p 111

[84]Idem, p 114

most important is the question raised by this researcher asking whether victim participation is as useful for victims as it should be considering the delay that victims have to patiently wait until their application for participation is decided upon,[85] but also their extent of participation if it meets the expectation of a restorative justice.

In the same line, Christine H. Chung reiterates that the Rome Statute grants to victims the right to participate to the ICC proceedings as "participants" and not as "parties."[86] She further highlights the fact that victims legal representatives are amongst voices doubting the workability of the ICC participation scheme[87] stressing how the current participation framework might have downplayed the proper assessment of how meaningful has the victim participation been in comparison to energy devoted to the granting of the status of victims, [88] considering that at the end, it remains unlikely that even successful applicants might never make it to address the Court and tell their story.[89]

Whereas di Giuseppo Zago analyses victims participation in the light of the Francis Muthaura and Uhuru Kenyatta cases highlighting that contrary to the reasoning of the Chamber, normally, it is after a victim has met the general criteria set by the Rule 85 of the RPE that it could be analyzed if such victim has a specific interest or rather a personal interest as described by article 68(3) of the Rome Statute, and not otherwise as the Chamber did.[90] Noteworthy saying that Zago's position is supported by the reasoning of the Trial Chamber I in the Decision on Victims participation.[91]

Furthermore the author stresses that if the Francis Muthaura and Uhuru Kenyatta reasoning would be adopted, not only does it reduces the involvement of judges in the status determination process which isn't the spirit of the ICC legal regime, but it also creates two types of victims of whom status had been

---

[85]Idem, p 125

[86]Christine H. Chung. 2008. Victims' Participation at the International Criminal Court: Are Concessions of the Court Clouding the Promise? In 6 *Northwestern Journal of International Human Rights 3*. p 465

[87]Idem p 463

[88]Idem p 509

[89]Idem p 513

[90]di Giuseppe Zago. 2014. The Role of Victims at the International Criminal Court: Legal Challenges from the Tension between Restorative and Retributive Justice. in *Diritto Penale Contemporaneo*. pp 8-9

[91]Thomas Lubanga Trial Chamber I, Decision on Victim's Partcipation of 18.01.2008 para 86

thoroughly established and a second type of victims whose claim has not been verified.[92] Perhaps the question of the rights of the accused should not be overlooked in the event that they are to face a group of victims whose claim to be victims has not been scrutinised and who are not even identifiable.[93]

Without the pretence of having extensively reviewed the current litterature on the question of victims' participataion at the ICC, a pertinent question on whether allowing victims an extensive participation is in interest of justice, fair and efficient trial and even in interest of victims themselves,[94] seems recurrent.

Thus Charles Trumbull argues that victims are not likely to benefit from the right to participate, and, more importantly, that their participation places costs on other groups of victims.[95] Indeed, after having brought out arguments of various sides and those of the supporters and the critics of the victim participation, the authors go on to question how would participation in international proceedings further victims' interest.

This author affirms that the truth telling process validates the victims experience and permits them to heal. However much as he agrees the reasons for allowing victims to participate in domestic trials-rehabilitation, reparations and more effective prosecutions cannot justify victims participation in an international context, he argues that if participation can be therapeutic, its effect will be significantly lessened due to the large number of victims who choose to participate in international criminal proceedings.

As already discussed, he questions whether victims participation may aid the Prosecution as he cautions against the unquestioned assumption that increased participation is in victims' best interests.[96]

In response to the previous query, using the cases of Banda and Jerbo in the Sudan situtaion, Emily Haslam and Rod Edmunds rather demonstrate how victims' interests can be so drastically opposed amongst themselves let alone as opposed to the Prosecution.[97]

---

[92]di Giuseppe Zago. 2014. The Role of Victims at the International Criminal Court: Legal Challenges from the Tension between Restorative and Retributive Justice. in *Diritto Penale Contemporaneo.* pp 8-9

[93]Idem

[94]Elisabeth Baumgartner. 2008. Aspects of victim participation in the proceedings of the International Criminal Court, *90 International Review of the Red Cross 870.* p 410

[95]Charles P. Trumbull. 2008. The Victims of Victim Participation in International Criminal Proceedings, *Michigan Journal of international law 29.* p 779

[96]Idem, p 826

[97]Emily Haslam and Rod Edmunds.2013. Victim Participation, Politics and the Construction of

In conclusion, after having highlighted the application process and various procedural rights granted to victims at various stages, Judge Van den Wyngaert also questions how meaningful the ICC victims' participatory regime can be.

She clarifies, unlike the truth and reconciliation commission, that the Court is not a forum where victims could come to express their grief and expose their feelings, the Court not being an appropriate forum for victims to express their feelings, as this would detract from the serenity of the trial and would not serve a useful purpose from the perspective of a criminal proceeding. [98]

Given such circumstances Judge Van de Wyngaert questions whether the legal representation can achieve anything more than symbolic representation and how meaningful can such representation be.[99]

She further draws attention on the prosecutorial selectivity policy which might have a negative impact on reconciliation considering that there may be certain victims belonging to different sides of a conflict without understanding the legal intricacies of the Prosecutor's decision may be left wondering why other victims can be granted participatory rights and not them. Thus her caution whether it might not be too much expectations from the ICC to be retributive and restorative at the same time. [100]

However Anaradha Saibaba Rajesh, after having highlighted how victims of crimes have been re-victimized by being ignored and neglected in the criminal justice system, through his work studies the point of convergence and divergence between the ICC and restorative justice,[101] and concludes that: "Empowerment of victims is ensured through their active participation in the prosecutions and trial processes."[102]

Victims at the International Criminal Court: Reflections on Proceedings in Banda and Jerbo, *Melbourne Journal of International Law 14.*

[98]Christine Van den Wyngaert. 2011. Victims before International Criminal Courts: Some Views and Concerns of an ICC Trial Judge. *44 Case W. Res. J. Int'l L. 475.* p 489

[99]Idem

[100]Idem, 492

[101]Idem, 123

[102]Anuradha Saibaba Rajesh. 2009. Victims in the International Criminal Court: Vindicated or Vanquished, *9 ISIL Y.B. Int'l Human. & Refugee L. 120.* p 142

2

HISTORICAL AND CONTEMPORARY PERSPECTIVES

1. Victims' Participation in early International Tribunals

1.1. International Military Tribunal of Nuremberg

At the outmost, it should be said that victims played a minimal role and their participation in the Nuremberg International Military Tribunal proceedings was nearly nonexistent.[103] Might that be because the proceedings at the Nuremberg Tribunal were mainly influenced by the adversarial system?[104]

However articles 15[105] and 17[106] of the Nuremberg IMT-Statute, which could be considered as the input of Russian and French delegations at the negotiations of the London Treaty, timidly allows respectively the Chief

---

[103]Sam Garkawe. 2006. The role and rights of victims at the Nuremberg International Military Tribunal, in *Die Nürnberger Prozesse Völkerstrafrecht seit 1945*. K.G. Saur München. p 86. Indeed, Professor William Schabas says: At Nuremberg, only a few victims actually testified, and their role was insignificant" See William A. Schabas. 2010. *The International Criminal Court, A commentary on the Rome Statute*. Oxford University Press. p 822

[104]Antonio Cassese. 2008. *International Criminal Law*. Second Edition. Oxford University Press. p 366

[105]Art. 15 (c) of the Nuremberg IMT Statute according to which: "The Chief Prosecutor shall individually, and acting in collaboration with one another, also undertake the following duties: c. the preliminary examination of all necessary witnesses and of the defendant…"

[106]Art. 17 (a) of the Nuremberg IMT Statute provided that: "The Tribunal shall have the power a. to summon witnesses to the trial and to require their attendance and testimony and to put questions to them."

Prosecutor and the Tribunal to call upon witnesses and to put questions to them.

Thus, the Tribunal's records indicate that the General Secretary's Office received a huge number of applications from different detention places, majority of whom were prisoners of war[107] who were willing to testify. Obviously, some witnesses testified against the accused; however, most of them were rather disculpatory. Nevertheless, it remains noticeable that victims were not called to give their testimony.

1.2. International Military Tribunal for the Far East

Not surprisingly, The International Military Tribunal for the Far East which was created in 1946 for the purposes of punishing Far Eastern war criminals for crimes of crimes against peace, conventional war crimes and crimes against humanity,[108] seems to have followed the same pattern as its Nuremberg predecessor.

Indeed the two tribunals' conceptual framework present similarities.[109] Hence, victims never played any role in the Tokyo proceedings as they never played any significant role in the Nuremberg Tribunal.

Like the Nuremberg tribunal, according to article 11 of the Charter of the Tokyo Tribunal: "The tribunal shall have the power [...] to summon witnesses to trial, to require them to attend and testify and to question them." Whereas article 5 providing for the Tribunal's jurisdiction over person and offenses said that: "the tribunal shall have the power to try and punish Far Eastern war criminals who as individuals or as members of organisations are charged with offences which include crimes against peace."

Thus, the Tokyo Tribunal received a total of 416 witnesses and 779 affidavits.[110] Unfortunately, some allied governments put obstacles in the way

[107]Final Report on the Evidence of Witnesses for the Defense of Organizations Alleged to be Criminal, Heard Before a Commission Appointed by the Tribunal Pursuant to Paragraph 4 of the Order of the 13th of March, 1946 available at http://avalon.law.yale.edu/imt/naeve.asp According to the report, By the 26th of April, the total number of applications to be heard had reached the figure of 81,433. Members of the SS alone sent in a total of 58,597. When the time limit for affidavits was reached on August 5th, the total number of collective affidavits submitted was 313,213

[108]See Art. 5 of the Charter of the International Military Tribunal for the Far East

[109]John Pritchard. 1998. *The Tokyo Major War Crimes Trials*. The Edwin Mellen Press. p xxxix.

[110]Idem, p lvi

of potential witnesses who were prepared to testify on behalf for the defence.[111] However, much that little is known about the Tokyo trials,[112] some survivors of the Far East atrocities were able to appear as witness before the Tribunal[113] not as participants but as witnesses.

As said by Professor William Schabas, victims did not fare particularly well in the initial at prosecution before the international military tribunals at Nuremberg and Tokyo.[114] The great irony of war is that the more catastrophic and widespread its destructive consequences, the less likely that those caught in its path will ever be repaid for their injury.[115]

2. Victims Participation and National Legal Systems

As discussed earlier, early international tribunals might have been influenced by the adversarial legal system of common law countries which might have negatively contributed to the role paid by victims before these courts.[116] If one considers the ICC's legal regime having borrowed[117] from accusatorial and inquisitorial systems,[118] this section intends to study the extent to which the two legal systems have contributed to the participation of victims before the International Criminal Court. However it does not intend to enter "the full-scale debate on the epistemic debate on adversarial-

[111]Idem, p lvii

[112]Solis Horwitz. 1950. The Toky Trial. In *International Conciliation, Carnegie Endowment for International Peace*. p 475

[113]John L. Ginn. Sugamo Prison. 1992. *Tokyo: An Account of the Trial and Sentencing of Japanese War Criminal in 1948 by a U.S. Participant.* McFarland& Company. p 52

[114]William A. Schabas. 2007. *An Introduction to the International Criminal Court.* Third Edition. Cambridge University Press. p325

[115]Roger P. Alford. 2006. War Reparations, the Holocaust, and the ICC in *Die Nürnberger Prozesse Völkerstrafrecht seit 1945*. K.G. Saur München. p 284

[116]Mark A. Drumbl. 2007. *Atrocity, Punishment, and International Law.* Cambridge University Press. p 42 as he argues that: "Indeed until recently, victims have not played a central role. This might be a result of the domination of the adversarial approach at the ICTR, ICTY and SCSL."

[117]Mauro Politi and Federica Gioia. 2002. *The Criminal Procedure before the International Criminal Court: Main Features,* in The Law and Practice of International Courts and Tribunals. p 115

[118]Human Right Watch. 2008. *Courting History, The Landmark International Criminal Court's First Years.*

inquisitorial dichotomy."[119] It rather focuses on the synthesis[120] of the two systems and its consequences on victims' rights before the ICC after it has discussed the role of victims in the Islamic legal system.

The Islamic legal system might not have influenced a lot the drafting of the ICC Statute provisions relevant to the participation of victims before the ICC; however the role played by victims in the Islamic system is negligible.

2.1. Victims' Role in the Islamic Legal System

Much of that practice might not be consistent in all countries applying the Islamic legal system; it remains however true that victims play an important role during criminal trials, especial for crimes committed against an individual.

Indeed though to a limited extend, certain crimes, including offences against a person, for instance intentional injury and homicide, are considered matters to be settled between the offender and victim.[121] In this case, the victim has a say in the decision to be taken by the court,[122] and the victims' pardon is one of the reasons for extinguishing the penalty.[123]

However as far as procedure is concerned there is no legal obligation to testify in certain cases, and this could result in the lack of sufficient evidence which might cause termination of proceedings. However, this applies to

[119]John Jackson. 2009. Finding the Best Epistemic fit for International Criminal Tribunals, Beyond the Adversarial-Inquisitorial Dichotomy, in *Journal of International Criminal Justice 7.* p 19

[120]King, F. and La Rosa A. *International Criminal Tribunal for the Former Yugoslavia: Current Survey-the Jurisprudence of the Yugoslavia Tribunal:1994-1996,* as cited by Mark Findlay. 2001. Synthesis in Trial Procedures? The Experience of International Criminal Tribunals, in *50 The International and Comparative Law Quarterly 1.* p 28.

[121]Christie S. Warren "Islamic Criminal Law". In *Oxford Bibliographies Online*, http://www.oxfordbibliographiesonline.com/ last consulted on 02.07.2020

[122]According to Ciprian-Vasile Maftei "They may require the same punishment as the act, a financial compensation (dyieh) or may decide that the perpetrator be forgiven (Art. 261) (Example of Koran: Chapter IV, Verse 24: "that, who accidentally kills another believer must give a ransom to the victim's relatives, unless he is forgiven...") see Ciprian-Vasile Maftei, The Sanctions of the Islamic Criminal law: Aspects Regarding Penalties of the Criminal Law of the Islamic Republic of Iran. Religion and Tradition vs. Observing Human Rights, in *Curentul Juridic,* p145 available at http://revcurentjur.ro/arhiva/attachments_201003/recjurid103_13F.pdf last consulted on 02.07.2020

[123]M. Akida, Criminal law in Nathalie Bernard-Maugiron and Baudouin Dupret. 2002. *Egypt and its Laws.* Kluwer Law International. p 42

crimes that require either a formal complaint or an eyewitness testimony.[124]

Generally speaking, three sets of crimes exist under Islamic criminal law. The first being constituted by crimes or offences against God, for which the punishment is mandatory as provided by the Koran; the Public prosecution is thus entrusted with the enforcement duties over such crimes.

The second category is constituted by crimes against individuals. The State allows its judicial institutions as a means through which the victim could seek justice including punishment of the offender and/or financial compensation *"diyya."* The proceeding and the sentencing depends heavily of the victims wishes. It is at this point that the victims pardon becomes the determining factor in the Islamic criminal law.

In the controversial Raymond Davis case, it was reported that the families of the two victims were "coerced" to accept financial compensation in return for pardoning the accused.[125] The acceptance of the "blood money" compensation was considered as having pardoned the accused person and resulted into the accused' s acquittal.[126]

The third category of crimes seem unspecified and are left to the discretion of the court.[127] The law does not have strict provisions on this category of crimes.

2.2. Civil Law System

In inquisitorial criminal proceedings, victims have a central role. They may play an important part in the prosecutor's decision to charge or not to charge the accused. They may request the court to review and reverse of the prosecutor's decision to charge or not to charge. In some cases, they are parties to the proceedings with full participatory rights to examine witnesses, file written submission, and request hearings.[128]

---

[124]Abd ar-Rahman I. *Doi, Shari'ah, Islamic Law.* Ta-Ha Publishers Ltd. p 342

[125]See BBC News, Pakistan Anger over release of CIA Man Raymond Davis, available at http://www.bbc.co.uk/news/world-south-asia-12769714?print=true last consulted on 02.07.2020

[126]See BBC News, CIA Contractor Ray Davis Freed over Pakistan Killings, available at http://www.bbc.co.uk/news/word-south-asia-12757244?print=true

[127]Matthew Lippman. 1989. Islamic Criminal Law and Procedure: Religious Fundamentalism v. Modern Law, *12 Boston College International and Comparative Law Review 1.* p 38

[128]Gideon Boas et al. 2011. *International Criminal Procedure, International Criminal Law Practitioner Library.* Cambridge University Press. p 306

Indeed the absence of victims during criminal trial is due to the fact that the adversarial system tends to separate criminal proceedings from civil proceedings as civil claims must be instituted after the criminal trial has ended, which is not the case for inquisitorial system which can merge the criminal and civil proceedings.[129]

Records of the *travaux preparatoires* indicate that this aspect was raised by the Japanese delegation which vehemently the opposed British and French positions. Japan said that it accepted the principle of reparations, but had legal difficulties with the idea of reparations because under the common law system, damages are given in civil rather than criminal proceedings.[130]

2.3. Common Law System

In adversarial criminal proceedings victims are subjects of the proceedings. They are not parties to the proceedings, have no authority to direct the investigation or affect the charging decision or procedure,[131]or determine the conduct of the judicial proceedings. The proceedings are party-driven and they pit prosecutor against defendant, leaving no role for a third party.

The victims' role in most common law jurisdictions is thus limited to that of a witness. As a witness, the victim can only speak if called by the prosecution (or defence) and can only answer questions that are posed to them.[132]

2.4. The Hybrid Nature of Victim's Participation at the ICC

As said by Professor Antinio Casesse, the adversarial and the inquisitorial systems cannot be considered watertight categories.[133] Indeed ways of

---

[129]Antonio Cassese. 2008. International Criminal Law. Second Edition. Oxford University Press. p 361 It is equally important to note that though considered from a different perspective the ICC being a Court of public character the difficulties that it raises when addressing victims claims which are private in character might be answered in the fact that when considered from the inquisitorial point of view nothing would prevent a criminal court to address issues of private nature namely compensation for victims as asked by Liesbeth Zegveld, Liesbeth Zegveld. 2010. Victims' Reparations Claims and International Criminal Court, in *Journal of International Criminal Justice 8*. p 100

[130]See OTR, ICC, Vol. 1, Part 2

[131]Gideon Boas et al. 2011. *International Criminal Procedure, International Criminal Law Practitioner Library.* Cambridge University Press. p 305

[132]Charles P. Trumbull. 2008. The Victims of Victim Participation in International Criminal Proceedings, *Michigan Journal of International Law 29.* p 781

[133]Antonio Cassese. 2008. *International Criminal Law.* Second Edition. Oxford University Press. p 353

developing proof and argument remains different in the two systems.[134] For instance, from its nature the adversarial system does not consider victims to be part of the criminal proceedings.[135] They may appear before the court though, but merely as witnesses.

Whereas the role assigned to victims by the Rome Statute seems to echo the one vested in the *partie civile*,[136] which is familiar to the inquisitorial system.[137] One may still submit that the concept of victims in the inquisitorial system and witnesses in the accusatorial system have both inspired the ICC legal regime.

When a victim status is granted to an applicant for the purposes of taking fully part to the proceedings, such procedure seems to be close to the *partie civile* in the inquisitorial system, and when a victim is rather participating to the proceeding as a witness without other procedural rights, they could be seen as victim-witness according to the accusatorial system.

3. Ad Hoc Tribunals

3.1. International Criminal Tribunal for Former Yugoslavia

The UN Security Council Resolution 827 adopted on the 25 May 1993 providing for the Statute of the International Criminal Tribunal for the former Yugoslavia, as amended from time to time provides in its Art. 22 that:

> The International Tribunal shall provide in its rules of procedure and evidence for the protection of victims and witnesses. Such protection measures shall include, but shall not be limited to, the conduct of in camera proceedings and the protection of the victim's identity.[138]

[134]Manoj Kumar Sinha. 2003. Are European Inquisitorial and Adversarial Criminal Justice Systems Converging? In *43 Indian Journal of International Law 1*. p 547

[135]Sam Garkawe. 2006. The Role and Rights of Victims at the Nuremberg International Military Tribunal, in *Die Nürnberger Prozesse Völkerstrafrecht seit 1945*, K.G. Saur München. p 91

[136]La partie civile désigne la victime, qui se pretend lésée par une infraction pénale, pour participer à l'exercice de l'action publique devant les jurisdictions répressives see Emmanuel Vergé Ed. 1969. *Répertoire de Droit Pénal et de Procédure Pénale, „partie civile,"* Tome III. Dalloz p 2

[137]Mauro Politi and Federica Gioia. 2002. the criminal procedure before the international criminal court: main features, in *The Law and Practice of International Courts and Tribunals 5*. p120

[138]Art. 22 of the Statute of the ICTY

According to Rule 34(A) of the Rules of Procedure and Evidence of the ICTY:

> There shall be set up under the authority of the Registrar a Victims and Witnesses Section consisting of qualified staff to:
> (i) recommend protective measures for victims and witnesses in accordance with Article 22 of the Statute; and
> (ii) provide counseling and support for them, in particular in cases of rape and sexual assault.[139]

Obviously, the role of victims as contemplated from the ICTY legal regime is limited only to their role as witnesses.[140] This regime provides for protective measures and setting up of modality of victim's participation to the trial, however only as witnesses when they are called either by the Chambers, the Prosecutor or the defence.[141]

Thus, victims' participatory rights before the ICTY being limited to their participation as witnesses, their compensatory rights according to Rule 98 *ter* B[142] in connection with Rule 105 are also limited to "a possibility that in case it is concluded by the trial chamber that unlawful taking of property was associated with the crime and a specific finding to that effect was made in the judgment, the trial chamber may order the restitution either of the property or the proceeds as appropriate."[143]

Needless to say that calls for a more effective compensation mechanism[144] at the ICTY, seem to have remained unanswered. Perhaps this is what led the President of the International Criminal Tribunal for the Former Yugoslavia in

---

[139]Rule 34(A) of the Rules of Procedure and Evidence of the ICTY

[140]http://www.icty.org/sections/Outreach/VoiceoftheVictims

[141]Holger-C. Rohne, The victims and witnesses section at the ICTY, an interview with Wendy Lobwein, Max-Planck-Institut für ausländisches und internationals Strafrecht, 2003, available at http://www.mpicc.de/shared/data/pdf/the_victims_and_witness_section_at_the_icty_(rohne).pdf last consulted on 02.07.2020

[142]According to Rule 98 ter (B): "If the Chamber finds the accused guilty of a crime and concludes from the evidence that unlawful taking of property by the accused was associated with it, it shall make a specific finding to that effect in its judgment. The Trial Chamber may order restitution as provided in Rule 105."

[143]Theo van Boven. 2009. Victims' Rights and Interest in the International Criminal Court, in *The Legal Regime of the International Criminal Court, Essays in Honour of Professor Igor Blishchenko.* Martinus Nojhoff Publishers. p 898.

[144]See for instance Statement by Judge Patrick Robinson, President of the International Criminal Tribunal for the former Yugoslavia to the Security Council on 3 December 2009, p 2

his Address to the U.N.G.A. of Oct. 8, 2009 to state that: "I fear that failure by the international community to address the needs of victims of the conflicts that occurred in the former Yugoslavia will undermine the Tribunal's efforts to contribute to long term peace and stability in the region."[145] A statement, which might have influenced discussions on the role of victims during the Rome Diplomatic Conference of the ICC.

3.2. International Criminal Tribunal for Rwanda

As for the ICTY, the ICTR might have been created along retributive lines.[146] This made it more concerned about punishing criminals of the atrocities they were accused of, without being more focused on the victims.

Indeed Art. 21 of the ICTR Statute mentions the word victim[147] leaves the victims participatory right to be governed by the rules of procedures; however they can only take part to the proceedings as witnesses.[148] As for their right to compensation, it is limited to restitution of property that might have been unlawfully taken from the victim on whom the Court should have sentenced the offender.[149]

Such provision could not have worked as most of the accused who were mainly former governmental officers soon after their arrest declared themselves indigents and relied on the Tribunal system for payment of their defence fees, most of their assets having been dissimulated so as not to create any funds to compensate victims.

Furthermore, if victims' compensation is limited to the restitution of their properties taken from them unlawfully, crimes which do not involve property rights will obviously remain beyond any possibility of compensation. Thus, it could be concluded that the UN ad hoc tribunals restricted the participation of victims as witnesses and its compensation mechanism was inadequate.

---

[145]Judge Patrick Robinson, President of the International Criminal Tribunal for the Former Yugoslavia, Address to the U.N.G.A., The Hague, Oct. 8, 2009

[146]Ilaria Bottigliero. 2004. *Redress for Victims of Crimes under International Law.* Martinus Nijhoff Publishers. p 211

[147]Art. 21 of the ICTR Statute which seems to reproduce Art. 22 of the ICTY saying: "The International Tribunal for Rwanda shall provide in its Rules of Procedure and Evidence for the protection of victims and witnesses. Such protection measures shall include, but shall not be limited to, the conduct of in camera proceedings and the protection of victim's identity."

[148]Rule 75 of the Rules of Procedure and Evidence of the ICTR which provided for measures for the protection of victims and witnesses

[149]Rule 88 (C) of the Rules of Procedure and Evidence of the ICTR

4. Special Courts

4.1. Extraordinary Chambers within the Courts of Cambodia

The Extraordinary Chambers in the Courts of Cambodia, ECCC, was created by the Law on the Establishment of the Extraordinary Chambers in the Courts of Cambodia for the Prosecution of Crimes Committed during the Period of Democratic Kampuchea.[150] The ECCC is part of the Cambodian judicial system[151]though with international assistance.

The Extraordinary Chambers is subject of an agreement between the United Nations and the Royal Government of Cambodia.[152] It is composed of both Cambodian judges and international judges.[153] The Extraordinary Chambers apply both international laws and Cambodian laws.[154]

It is interesting to note that the Law of the Establishment of the Extraordinary Chambers does not even mention anywhere the word victim. However, its internal rules have provided for a wide range of rights for victims as discussed below.

Indeed, the participatory status before the Extraordinary Chambers is granted by the Co-Investigating Judges as provided for by rule 22 (2) the Internal Rules. It is required for the victim who wishes to participate as *partie civile* to fulfill the following conditions:

> (i) be clearly identified, and
> (ii) demonstrate as a direct consequence of at least one of the crimes alleged against the Charged person, that he or she has suffered physical, material or psychological injury upon which a claim of collective and moral reparation might be based[155]

---

[150]The Law on the Establishment of the Extraordinary Chambers in the Courts of Cambodia for the Prosecution of Crimes Committed during the Period of Democratic Kampuchea, Unofficial translation by the Council of Jurists and the secretariat of the task force, revised 26 August 2007, available at www.eccc.gov.kh last consulted on 02.07.2020

[151]Guido Acquaviva. 2008. New Paths in International Criminal Justice? The Internal Rules of the Cambodian Extraordinary Chambers. In *Journal of International Criminal Justice 6*. p 130

[152]Agreement between the United Nations and the Royal Government of Cambodia concerning the prosecution under Cambodian law of crimes committed during the period of Democratic Kampuchea.

[153]Art. 3 (1) of the Agreement.

[154]Art. 9 of the Agreement, See Chapter II of the Law on the establishment of the Extraordinary Chambers

[155]Rule 23 bis (1)

Theoretically, once the status of victim has been granted to the applicant as *partie civile,* they participate fully to the proceedings. However, as it has been demonstrated by Kate Gibson and Daniella Rudy, the practice of the Extraordinary Chambers is not consistent on the extent to which such victims should participate to the proceeding.[156]

For instance, during the proceeding of its 31st trial day, defence counsel expressed his concern over the nature of the question that were being asked by the *partie civile* as the defence council wished for the *partie civile* to be urged to concentrate on what is of direct relevance to the victims, and not to reopen a prosecution submission.[157]

After having heard the *partie civile* lawyer who based his claim on their role to support the prosecution,[158] the Extraordinary Chambers deliberated on the issue and allowed the *partie civile'* s lawyers to question the accused in order to support the alleged prosecution.[159]

Interestingly, during the proceedings on its 66th day, though not exactly in the same context, the issue was raised again as the Extraordinary Chambers had to give a ruling as to whether civil parties are allowed to question the accused and the witnesses called to testify at the part of the hearing that is entitled, according to the Scheduling Order?[160] The Chamber decided that the *parties civile* were not allowed to ask questions of the accused or of the witnesses.[161] Thus the unpredictability nature of the Extraordinary Chambers decision on the role of victims might be considered its biggest criticism.

---

[156]Kate Gibson and Daniella Rudy. 2009. A New Model of International Criminal Procedure? The Progress of the Duch Trial at the ECCC.In *Journal of International Criminal Justice7.* pp-1015-1016

[157]Extraordinary Chambers in the Court of Cambodia, Transcript of Trial Proceedings-Kaing Guek Eav „Duch" Public Case File No001/18-07-2007-ECCC/TC, 22 June 2009, 0905H, Trial Day 31, pp 91-92

[158]Rule 23 (1) (a)

[159]Extraordinary Chambers in the Court of Cambodia, Transcript of Trial Proceedings-Kaing Guek Eav „Duch" Public Case File No001/18-07-2007-ECCC/TC, 22 June 2009, 0905H, Trial Day 31, pp 98

[160]Extraordinary Chambers in the Court of Cambodia, Transcript of Trial Proceedings-Kaing Guek Eav „Duch" Public Case File No001/18-07-2007-ECCC/TC, 27 August 2009, 0905H, Trial Day 66, p 74

[161]Id.,

4.2. Special Tribunal for Lebanon

The Special Tribunal for Lebanon was created as response to the request of the Government of the Republic of Lebanon to the United Nations to establish a tribunal of an international character to try all those who are alleged responsible the attack of 14 February 2005 resulting in the death of former Lebanese Prime Minister Rafiq Hariri and in the death or injury of other persons.[162] It is composed of Lebanese and international personnel. According to Art. 2 of its Statute, the Tribunal applies Lebanese laws.[163]

Rule 2 of the Rules of Procedure and Evidence define the concept of victim as "a natural person who has suffered physical, material or mental harm as a direct result of an attack within the Tribunal's jurisdiction,[164] thus legal persons are excluded from such status.[165] Victims' participatory right is provided for by Art. 17 of the Statute according to which:

> Where the personal interest of the victims are affected, the Special Tribunal shall permit their views and concerns to be presented and considered at stages of the proceedings determined to be appropriate by the Pre-Trial Judge or the Chamber and in a manner that is not prejudicial to or inconsistent with the rights of the accused and a fair and impartial trial. Such views and concerns may be presented by the legal representatives of the victims where the Pre-Trial Judge or the Chamber considers it appropriate.[166]

However the participation of victims to the proceedings must be authorised by the Pre-Trial Chamber or the Trial Chamber, and it starts at the trial stage.[167] Thus, victims cannot participate at the investigation stage as they can only be

---

[162]Art. 1 of Agreement between the United Nations and the Lebanese Republic on the establishment of a Special Tribunal for Lebanon annex to the Security Council Resolution 1757 of 30 May 2007

[163]Art. 2 of the Statute of the Special Tribunal for Lebanon attached to the Security Council Resolution 1757 of 30 May 2007

[164]Rule 2 of the Rule of Procedure and Evidence of the Special Tribunal for Lebanon

[165]Special Tribunal for Lebanon, Information Guide on Victims Participation in the Proceedings of the Special Tribunal for Lebanon para. 15

[166]Art. 17 of the Statute of the Special Tribunal for Lebanon attached to the Security Council Resolution 1757 of 30 May 2007

[167]Rule 87 (A), (B) of the Rules of Procedure and Evidence

allowed to take part in proceedings after the indictment has been confirmed.[168] Another distinguishing feature of the Tribunal is that it cannot provide for compensation of victims; however based on the decision of the Special Tribunal and pursuant to the relevant national legislation, a victim may bring a claim to a national court or other competent body to obtain compensation.[169]

---

[168]Jérome de Hamptinne. 2010. Challenges raised by Victims' Participation in the Proceedings of the Special Tribunal for Lebanon, in *Journal for International Criminal Justice 8*. p 166

[169]Art. 25 of the Statute of the Special Tribunal for Lebanon attached to the Security Council Resolution 1757 of 30 May 2007

3

VICTIMS' PARTICIPATION AT THE PRE-TRIAL STAGE

1. Procedural Status at the Investigation Stage

Victims' participation at the investigation phase might be one of issues on which the jurisprudence of the ICC seemed to be the most inconsistent in its early cases. As said by Bridie McAsey: "One of the most controversial aspects of victim participation has been the approach of several chambers in allowing victims to participate at the investigation stage of proceedings."[170]

A careful reading of articles 15(3) and 68(3) might give a hint on the source of such discrepancy within the jurisprudence of the ICC. On the one hand, investigations conducted by the Prosecutor are governed by Art. 15 of the Statute, on the other, as already said, participation of victims is generally provided under Art. 68 (3).

According to Art. 15(3) of the Statute makes reference to victims providing that:

> If the Prosecutor concludes that there is a reasonable basis to proceed with an investigation, he or she shall submit to the Pre-Trial Chamber a request for authorization of an investigation, together with any supporting material collected. Victims may make representations to the Pre-Trial Chamber, in accordance with the Rules of Procedure and Evidence

---

[170]Bridie McAsey. 2010. Victim Participation at the International Criminal Court and its Impact on Procedural Fairness, *Australian International Law Journal*. p 112

Already Art. 15(2) of the Statute provides that: "The Prosecutor shall analyse the seriousness of the information received. For this purpose, he or she may seek additional information from States, organs of the United Nations, intergovernmental or non-governmental organisations, or other reliable sources that he or she deems appropriate..." Certainly, the prosecution considers victims[171] as one of the reliable sources who can participates to its work by giving information about the crimes they allegedly suffered.[172]

Furthermore, when the Prosecutor decides to initiate an investigation *moto propio*, according to Rule 50(1) of the Rules, the Prosecutor must notify victims, known to him or her or to the Victims and Witnesses Unit, or their legal representatives,[173] for the purposes of enabling them to make their representations in accordance with the above-cited Art. 15(3).

Early practice of the Court demonstrates that under Art. 15(3) victims were not merely permitted to make submissions. Such submissions included factual evidence on various crimes, charged and/or uncharged crimes. They were equally entitled to be informed of the Chamber's decision, and were even granted leave to appeal against the chamber's decision.

Theoretically, at this point, the question of victims' participation has already raised controversies and such controversies are a result of the Statute itself which opens up for possible participation of victims under two separate legal provisions, which might not have been drafted in harmony.

Indeed, in its decision of 17.01.2006, the PTC found that: "Pursuant to article 68 (3) of the Statute, victims can participate only "[w]here the personal interests of the victims are affected". Whereas it noted that this criterion is not included in other provisions that give victims specific rights of participation, such as articles 15 (3) and 19 (3) of the Statute." [174]

One may submit that victims' submissions under Art. 15(3) amounts to victims' participation at the investigation phase even when no specific case has been instituted yet, hence the impossibility of establishing any nexus between the victim and the offender let alone the nexus between the victim and the crime charged against the offender hence the coining of the concept of victim of a situation[175] as hereunder discussed.

[171]Policy paper on victims' participation, ICC-OTP, 2010, p 14

[172]Charles P. Trumbull. 2008. The Victims of Victim Participation in International Criminal Proceedings. In *Michigan Journal of International Law 29*. p 791

[173]Rule 50 (1) of the Rules of Procedure and Evidence.

[174]ICC, Situation in the DRC, Public Redacted Version, Decision on the appeals for participation in the proceedings of VPRS 1, VPRS 2, VPRS 3, VPRS 4, VPRS 5 and VPRS 6, para 61-62

[175]ICC, Situation in the DRC, Public Redacted Version, Decision on the appeals for participation

2. Victims in a Situation or Victims in a Case

In the Thomas Lubanga case, the Trial Chamber I held that:

> During the trial stage of a case the right of victims to participate is principally dependent on whether their personal interests are affected in accordance with Article 68(3) of the Statute, and Rule 85 of the Rules which provides a definition of "victims" should be read in light of that Article. Rule 85 of the Rules does not have the effect of restricting the participation of victims to the crimes contained in the charges confirmed by Pre-Trial Chamber I, and this restriction is not provided for in the Rome Statute framework. Rule 85(a) of the Rules simply refers to the harm having resulted from the commission of a "crime within the jurisdiction of the Court" and to add the proposed additional element – that they must be the crimes alleged against the accused - therefore would be to introduce a limitation not found anywhere in the regulatory framework of the Court.[176]

However the same decision indicated further that:

> Victims have multiple and varied interests, but it is critical to emphasise and repeat that for victims to participate in this trial, these interests must relate to the evidence and the issues the Chamber will be considering in its investigation of the charges brought against Mr Thomas Lubanga Dyilo: the extent of the evidence and the issues to be considered by the Chamber during this trial are defined by the alleged crimes the accused faces.[177]

---

in the proceedings of VPRS 1, VPRS 2, VPRS 3, VPRS 4, VPRS 5 and VPRS 6, para 65. In whichthe PTC found that the Statute, the Rules of Procedure and Evidence and the Regulations of the Court draw a distinction between situations and cases in terms of the different kinds of proceedings...Situations are generally defined in terms of temporal, territorial and in some cases personal parameters, such as the situation in the territory of the Democratic Republic of the Congo entail the proceedings envisaged in the Statute to determine whether a particular situation should give rise to a criminal investigation as well as the investigation as such. Cases, which comprise specific incidents during which one or more crimes within the jurisdiction of the Court seem to have been committed by one or more identified suspects, entail proceedings that take place after the issuance of a warrant of arrest or a summons to appear.

[176]Thomas Lubanga, Trial Chamber I, Decision on victims' Participation of 18.01.2008, para 93

[177]Thomas Lubanga, Trial Chamber I, Decision on victims' Participation of 18.01.2008, para 97

Following the appeal of the Prosecutor and the Defence, the Appeals Chamber reversed the decision of the Trial Chamber after having acknowledged that rule 85 does not have the effect of restricting the participation of victims in the crimes charged. The Chamber affirmed that this provision must be read in context and in accordance with its object and purpose.[178] Thus the Appeals Chamber reversed the Trial Chamber I decision and ruled that:

> In relation to the object and purpose of rule 85, the Appeals Chamber considers that the rule does not have the effect of mandating participation of victims instead the object and purpose of rule 85 is to define who are victims. Thus, whilst the ordinary meaning of rule 85 does not per se, limit the notion of victims to the victims of the crimes charged, the effect of article 68 (3) of the Statute is that the participation of victims in the trial proceedings, pursuant to the procedure set out in rule 89 (1) of the Rules, is limited to those victims who are linked to the charges.[179]

The decision of the Appeals Chamber seems to have been followed by the lower chamber in other cases for instance the Dominic Ongwen case the PTC II held that:

> As interpreted in the case law of the Court, an applicant qualifies as a victim pursuant to the above provision provided that: (i) the identity of the applicant appears duly established; (ii) the event(s) described in the application for participation constitute(s) one or more crimes within the jurisdiction of the Court, with which the suspect is charged; and (iii) the applicant has suffered harm as a result of the crime(s) with which the suspect is charged.[180]

This position seems to have partially solved the problem; however, it falls short of explaining how victims could make their representations under Art. 15 (3).

---

[178]Thomas Lubanga, Appeals Camber, Judgment on the appeals of The Prosecutor and The Defence against Trial Chamber I's Decision on Victims' Participation of 18 January 2008, para 54

[179]Thomas Lubanga, Appeals Camber, Judgment on the appeals of The Prosecutor and The Defence against Trial Chamber I's Decision on Victims' Participation of 18 January 2008, para 58

[180]Dominic Ongwen, PTCII, Decision Establishing Principles on the Victims' Application Process, 04.03.15, para 18

3. Legal Representation under Art 15 (3)

According to rule 50(1) of the Rules, once the Prosecutor decides to proceed with an investigation, he or she has a duty to inform victims, known to him or her or to the Victims and Witnesses Unit, or their legal representatives of his or her decision for the purpuses of enabling them to make their representations.

In the event that the Prosecutor is of the opinion that any communication addressed directly to certain victims might endanger them or interfer with the integrity of the investigation, the Rules allow the prosecutor to inform the general public even by way of a public notice published through whatever means reaches the widest audience.[181]

Though rule 50(1) of the Rules does not mention rule 85 which defines the concept of victims, this rule might be understood as to allow victims who have not been screened by any chamber to make their legal representations. However, such literal interpretation might run contrary to the whole spirit of the Statute, which rather grants deciding powers on the participation of victims to judges.

Considering that, as rule 89(1) of the Rules provides that in order to present their views and concerns, victims shall make written application to the Registrar, who shall refer the application to the relevant Chamber.[182] It would follow that the Prosecutor would notify victims known to him or her of his or her decision who then shall make their application to the Pre Trial Chamber through the Registrar requesting the Pre Trial Chamber to allow them to make their legal representations.

As noted in the situation in the Islamic Republic of Afghanistan, at this point no victim application is required to meet the nexus requirement between the harm and charged crime, any legal representation which did not meet at least the criteria set by Rule 85 of the Rules were not transmitted to the Pre Trial Chamber.[183] Thus victims remain under duty to demonstrate how their personal interests are affected so as to satisfy the requirements of Art. 68(3) of the Statute read jointly with rule 85 of the Rules.[184]

---

[181]Rule 50(1) of the Rules

[182]Rule 89(1) of the Rules

[183]PTC II, Situation in the Islamic Republic of Afghanistan, Decision Pursuant to Article 15 of the Rome Statute on the Authorisation of an Investigation into the Situation in the Islamic Republic of Afghanistan of 12.04.2019, on para 27, footnote 16

[184]Situation in The Republic of Kenya, PTC II, Decision on Victims' Participation in Proceedings Related to the Situation in the Republic of Kenya of 3. 11. 2010, para 8

It is insightful to note that the Pre Trial Chamber II Decision on Victims' Participation in Proceedings Related to the Situation in the Republic of Kenya of 3. 11. 2010 acknowledged that, unless the Statute allows expressis verbis for victims' participation at specific stages of the proceedings, their participation is governed by Art. 68(3) of the Statute.[185]

It then could be understood that the rights of victims to participate to proceedings at this stage is granted under Art. 15(3) however the exercise of such rights will depend on wheither the applicant meet the requements of Art. 68(3) of the Statute and Rule 85 of the Rules.

Considering that even at investigation stage any question that requires a judicial determination is deemed to be part of judicial proceedings, it follows that victims applications to make their legal representation according to Art. 15(3), might be their first step to partcipation to the proceedings; obviously such application would be successful to enable such victims to then proceed and make their representations.

Nevertheless when a victim is allowed to participate to proceedings at a certain level, that does not guarantee that such victim will automaticaly participate in other stages of the proceedings as the decision of PTC remains valid only at that particular stage of the procedeeings, as any intervention of a victim will require prior authorisation of the relevant Chamber, which is in turn guided by the relevant provisions.

It is in this line that in the situation in Darfur, the Appeals Chamber reversed three decisions of the Pre Trial Chamber I on victim participation at the investigation phase in which decisions the Pre Trial Chamber I had ruled that there was a possibility to have the status of victim authorised to participate generally in the investigation of a situation and its case related proceedings before the Pre-Trial Chamber.[186]

These decisions were reversed not because victims could not participate in the proceedings at the investigation phase, but because such participation was not given in a general format subject to the provisions of Art. 68(3)[187] as further discussed.

[185]Situation in The Republic of Kenya, PTC II, Decision on Victims' Participation in Proceedings Related to the Situation in the Republic of Kenya of 3. 11. 2010, para 7

[186]Situation in Sudan, Appeals Chamber, Judgment on victim participation in the investigation stage of the proceedings in the appeal of the OPCD against the decision of Pre-Trial Chamber I of 3 December 2007 and in the appeals of the OPCD and the Prosecutor against the decision of Pre-Trial Chamber I of 6 December 2007, 02.02.2009, paras 41 and 59

[187]Idem para 57

4. Participation to the Determination on Jurisdiction or Admissibility

Art. 19 (3) of the Statute provides that:

> The Prosecutor may seek a ruling from the Court regarding a question of jurisdiction or admissibility. In proceedings with respect to jurisdiction or admissibility, those who have referred the situation under article 13, as well as victims, may also submit observations to the Court.

Though the wording of Art. 19(3) seems to limit such participation to submission of observations, nothing prevents the Chamber from allowing victims for more participation beyond submission of observation. Such participation is left to the Chamber's determination.

Following the request of the Prosecutor made under Art. 19(3) seeking a ruling on the question of whether the International Criminal Court may exercise its jurisdiction over the alleged deportation of the Rohingya people from Myanmar to Bangladesh, (Situation in Bangladesh/Myanmar.), the Pre Trial Chamber I reviewed two submissions on the behalf of victims, namely, the Submissions on Behalf of the Victims Pursuant to Article 19(3) of the Statute submitted by Global Rights Compliance, and a second submission titled „Observations on behalf of victims from Tula Toli" was submitted by victims' legal representatives.

Though the first submission was titled as a submission done pursuant Art. 19(3) it further indicated that it was done pursuant Art. 19(3) or alternatively Art. 68(3)of the Statute.[188] The second submission rather elaborated more on the question of a victim's standing under Art.19(3) of the Statute, and procedural consideration concerning victims' participation as provided for by Rule 59 of the Rules.[189]

According to Rule 59(1) which provides for Participation in proceedings under Art. 19(3):

---

[188]ICC, Pre Trial Chamber I, Submissions on behalf of the Victims Pursuant to Article 19(3) of the Statute, 30.05.2018, para 3

[189]ICC, Pre Trial Chamber I, Observations on behalf of Victims from Tula Toli, 18.06.2018 paras 76-87

> For the purpose of article 19, paragraph 3, the Registrar shall inform the following of any question or challenge of jurisdiction or admissibility which has arisen pursuant to article 19, paragraphs 1, 2 and 3
> (a) Those who have referred a situation pursuant to article 13;
> (b) The victims who have already communicated with the Court in relation to that case or their legal representatives.

Interestingly, the Chamber found that the victims have standing to submit observations pursuant to article 68(3) of the Statute. Furthermore, the Chamber was of the view that rule 93 of the Rules gives it discretion to accept observations presented by victims on any issue and at any stage of the proceedings, whenever the Chamber finds it appropriate.[190] Rule 93 providing for views of victims or their legal representative stipulates that:

> A Chamber may seek the views of victims or their legal representatives participating pursuant to rules 89 to 91 on any issue, *inter alia*, in relation to issues referred to in rules 107, 109, 125, 128, 136, 139 and 191. In addition, a Chamber may seek the views of other victims, as appropriate.

In its reasoning, the Chamber said that it considered that the victims' personal interests were affected by the Request in view of the fact that their applications were linked to the alleged deportations from Myanmar to Bangladesh in August 2017 decision hence its decision to hear from the victims at this stage.[191]

It should be recalled that at this point the Chamber had not yet done any determination on the status of victims and that some victims who had formally applied for the status of victims had not yet received any response with respect to their status; nevertheless the Chamber exercising its discretionary powers to accept victims submissions considered their views on the question at hand.

---

[190]ICC, Pre Trial Chamber I, Decision on the "Prosecution's Request for a Ruling on Jurisdiction under Article 19(3) of the Statute," 6 September 2018, para 21

[191]Idem

1. Confirmation of Hearing

However, victims' participation in the confirmation hearing could be considered one of the most important procedural rights granted to the victims before the Pre Trial Chamber,[192] Art. 16, which governs the confirmation of hearing is silent about victims. However Rule 92 (3) of the Rules provides that: "In order to allow victims to apply for participation in the proceedings in accordance with rule 89, the Court shall notify victims regarding its decision to hold a hearing to confirm charges pursuant to article 61."

As indicated earlier, Rule 89 gives discretion to the relevant Chamber to decide on victims' participation as the Chamber deems necessary. Thus in the case of Bahar Idriss Abu Garda, the PTC I decided that "Pursuant to rule 89(1) of the Rules, the Chamber further considers that the victims' legal representatives are entitled to make opening and closing statements at the confirmation hearing."[193] Furthermore, pursuant rule 121 (10) of the Rules, victims or their legal representative who are participating to the confirmation of hearing have access to records kept by the Registrar.

For instance in the Thomas Lubanga case, victims were allowed to make opening and closing remarks during the confirmation hearing, though their views were limited within the framework of the charges brought by the Prosecution.[194] However, some victims complained about such limitations.

In the Jean-Pierre Bemba Gombo case,[195]the victims' legal representation gave a submission on the establishment of individual criminal responsibility of the accused person.

In the Mbarushimana Case, victims made a submission on the identification of the perpetrators. Indeed, when the Defence argued that "the identification of the perpetrators by the victims, usually based on the language spoken by

[192]Germain Katanga and Mathieu Ngudjolo Chui, Pre-Trial Chamber I, Decision on the Set of Procedural Rights Attached to Procedural Status of Victim at the Pre-Trial Stage of the Case, 13 May 2008, para 23

[193]Situation in Darfur, Sudan, Pre-Trial Chamber I, in the case of Prosecutor V. Bahar Idriss Abu Garda, Decision on victims' modalities of participation at the Pre-Trial Stage of the Case, of 06 October 2009, para. 19

[194]Transcript of the confirmation of hearing of 28 November 2006, p 97, Indeed as the victims legal representative clearly indicated, "the charges of the Prosecutor have disappointed some victims" p 86.

[195]Situation en RCA, La Chambre Préliminaire II, Observations conjointes des Representants legaux des victimes sur Ie Document amende contenant les charges depose Ie 30 mars 2009

the attackers, is often unreliable, since many different Kinyarwanda-speaking militias are active in the DRC and members of some groups deliberately concealed their identity."[196] The legal representative of victims challenged the merits of the defence arguments on various grounds including that their identification of the FDLR forces as the perpetrators was reliable since many of them are former hostages who had been living together with their offenders for weeks, and that the perpetrators themselves claimed to be FDLR members.[197]

It goes without saying that the right to participate to the confirmation of hearing entiles victims with other subsequent rights including attendance to hearing, the right to receive notifications of fillings and decisions of the Court, the filling of written submission and acess to some Court's records as hereunder discussion.

Victims' legal represenitive may attend the proceedings of the confirmation of charges hearing. This is in accordance to Rule 91(2) of the Rules which provides that; „A legal representative of a victim shall be entitled to attend and participate in the proceedings in accordance with the terms of the ruling of the Chamber and any modification thereof given under rules 89 and 90. This shall include participation in hearings...„

However if circumstances of the case dictates that hearing takes place in camera the Chamber has the discretion of deciding on the question of victims participation, which could be restricted to written observations or otherwise.

As far as notifications are concerned, Rule 92(5) provides for notification of fillings that:

---

[196] ICC-01/04-01/10-450, Defence written submissions Pursuant to the Oral Order of Pre-Trial Chamber I of 16September 2011 ("Defence Final Submissions"), paras 52-6., as quoted in ICC-01/04-01/10, Decision on confirmation of charges of Pre-Trial Chamber I of 16 December 2011, para 9

[197] ICC-01/04-01/10-446, « Observations de victimes autorisées à participer à la procédure au terme de l'audience de confirmation des charges retenues contre M. Callixte Mbarushimana » («First Victims Final Submissions»), para. 23 ; ICC-01/04-01/10-447, « Observations et «conclusions finales" aux fins de confirmation des charges retenues contre C:MBARUSHIMANA Par les 37 victimes en vertu de Varticle 68 alinéa 3 du Statut de Rome. En vertu de la jurisprudence ICC nnCC-01l04:-0iy07-474-tFRA ch.prél.du 13 mai 2008 par.127 à 133 » («Second Victims Final Submissions»), para. 8, as quoted in ICC-01/04 01/10, Decision on confirmation of charges of Pre-Trial Chamber I of 16 December 2011, para 11

> In a manner consistent with the ruling made under rules 89 to 91, victims or their legal representatives participating in proceedings shall, in respect of those proceedings, be notified by the Registrar in a timely manner of:
> (a) Proceedings before the Court, including the date of hearings and any postponements thereof, and the date of delivery of the decision;
> (b) Requests, submissions, motions and other documents relating to such requests, submissions or motions.

It needs to be stressed that Rule 92(5) (b) is of particular interest to victims considering that the submission and motions made by the victims are of essence to their participatory rights. Such right is however subject to a prior request addressed to the chamber, which will then grant leave to a particular victim or their legal representation to make their submission.

Subsequently Rule 92(6) provides for notifications of decisions saying that: "Where victims or their legal representatives have participated in a certain stage of the proceedings, the Registrar shall notify them as soon as possible of the decisions of the Court in those proceedings."

As far as access to the public record is concerned, Rule 121(10) of the Rules provides clearly that: „Subject to any restrictions concerning confidentiality and the protection of national security information, the record may be consulted by the Prosecutor, the person and victims or their legal representatives participating in the proceedings pursuant to rules 89 to 91.„ The legal representatives of victims may thus consult the record of proceedings at the Registry of the Court.

Other than specific provisions, which allow victims to actively participate in the proceedings, the Statute has instances where victims come into consideration albeit in a passive fashion. This is the case of Arts. 53(1) C and 57(3) C of the Statute and Rule 119 of the Rules

6. Participation when the Prosecutor decides not to investigate

Under Art. 53 (1) C, if the Prosecutor finds that there is no reasonable ground to proceed with an investigation, the Statute requires the Prosecution amongst other reasons to take into consideration the interests of victims, before determining that an investigation would not serve the best interests of justice.

Although Art 53 does not clarify the role of victims at this stage, rule 92(2) of the Rules provides that: "In order to allow victims to apply for participation in the proceedings in accordance with rule 89, the Court shall notify victims concerning the decision of the Prosecutor not to initiate an investigation or not to prosecute pursuant to article 53."

It then follows that the Chamber will exercise it discretion as to the extent and modality of participation of victims at this stage. As indicated by Professor William Schabas the presence of victim before the Pre Trial Chamber might be formed to ensure that when the prosecutor decides not to prosecute, s/he does this genuinely.[198]

7. Protective Measures

Art 57(3) C which provides for protective measures allows the Pre Trial Chamber to exercise its functions and if necessary to offer protection for victims and witnesses and to safeguard their privacy including their well-being, dignity, non disclosure of their identity...[199]

---

[198]William A. Schabas. 2004. An introduction to the international criminal court. Second Edition. Cambridge University Press. p172 see further Carsten Stahn. Héctor Olásolo. Kate Gibson. 2006. Participation of Victims in Pre-Trial Proceedings of the ICC. In *Journal of International Criminal Justice 4.* p 15

[199]Situation in the DRC, Prosecutor V. Thomas Lubanga, Trial Chamber I Decision inviting the parties' observations on applications for participation of a/0001/06 to a/0004/06, a/0047/06 to a/0052/06, a/0077/06, a/0078/06, a/0105/06, a/0221/06, a/0224/06 to a/0233/06, a/0236/06, a/0237/06 to a/0250/06, a/0001/07 to a/0005/07, a/0054/07 to a/0062/07, a/0064/07, a/0065/07, a/0149/07, a/0155/07, a/0156/07, a/0162/07, a/0168/07 to a/0185/07, a/0187/07 to a/0191/07, a/0251/07 to a/0253/07, a/0255/07 to a/0257/07, a/0270/07 to a/0285/07, and a/0007/08 of 6 May 2008 para 28 the chamber authorized the redaction of i) name of applicant ; ii) name of parents; iii) place of birth; iv) exact date of birth (year of birth shall not be redacted); v) tribe or ethnic group; vi) occupation; vii) current address; viii) phone number and email address; ix) name of other victims of, or of witnesses to, the same incident; x) identifying features of the injury, loss or harm allegedly suffered; xi) name and contact details of the intermediary assisting the victim in filing the application. See also Situation in Uganda Decision on legal representation, appointment of counsel for the defence, protective measures and time-limit for submission of observations on applications for participation a/0010/06, a/0064/06 to a/0070/06, a/0081/06 to a/0104/06 and a/0111/06 to a/0127/06 1 February 2007 para 21 and 22, see Situation in Darfur, Sudan, Pre-Trial Chamber I, Decision on Confidentiality Matters and Extension of Page Limit, 8 June 2007, p 4 see International Seminar on access of victims to the International Criminal Court, Report of workshops 29 of April, 1999 pp 9-10

Indeed, protective measures are further provided for under Art. 68 (1) of the Statute according to which the Court to take such protective measures particularly when dealing with traumatised victims or witnesses, children, elderly and victims of sexual and gender violence.[200] If the Chamber so decides, victims may also take part to the proceeding when the chamber considers taking such measures for their protection.[201]

Furthermore, protective measures may be taken to protect victims and/or to avoid degradation or alteration of such evidence. Thus when the Prosecutor considers that there is a serious risk that it might not be possible for the testimony to be taken subsequently, he or she may request the Pre-Trial Chamber to take such measures as may be necessary to ensure the efficiency and integrity of the proceedings.[202] Many reasons might justify such decision, including but not limited, to the security conditions that might later prove difficult for the court to access such evidence.[203]

8. Conditional Release

Rule 119(1) C of the Rules that provide for conditional release stipulates that: "The Pre-Trial Chamber may set one or more conditions restricting liberty, including the following: (c) The person must not contact directly or indirectly victims or witnesses." Such prohibition is understandably for the safety of victims and witnesses but could also ensure that evidence is not tampered with. While there is nothing required of the victim, it remains a relevant provision when one consider cases where victims have been threatened or even killed.

---

[200]Trial Chamber III, Prosecutor v. Jean-Pierre Bemba Gombo, Decision defining the status of 54 victims who participated at the pre-trial stage, and inviting the parties' observations on applications for participation by 86 applicants of 22 February 2010, para 24 Citing ICC-01/04-01/06-1119

[201]Situation in Uganda, Public redacted version, Decision on victim's application for participation a/ ....of 10 August 2007

[202]Rule 47 (2)

[203]Situation in Darfur, Pre-Trial Chamber I, Observations on issues concerning the protection of victims and the preservation of evidence in the proceedings on Darfur pending before the ICC, 25 August 2006; pp 10-11

Further, the same Rule 119(3) provides that:

> Before imposing or amending any conditions restricting liberty, the Pre-Trial Chamber shall seek the views of the Prosecutor, the person concerned, any relevant State and victims that have communicated with the Court in that case and whom the Chamber considers could be at risk as a result of a release or conditions imposed.

As indicated earlier the risk facing victims of crimes within the jurisdiction of the the ICC cannot be over empasised. It is important that such mechanism is put in place and further action are taken if necessary.

9. The Challenge of Numbers

Other than the challenge related to interpretation of various legal provisions, the Court has been faced by logistical challenges including some related to huge numbers of victims applying to participate to the proceedings and it subsequent delay in the determination of the status of victims. For instance in the Ntaganda case the registry assessed that it would need one year to process and submit victims' applications.[204]

Thus, the Court has kept on creating various mechanisms to shorten the process by various means including by creating a simplified procedure which allows a given group to make a joint application as a group. Such experience started with the Gbagbo case, in which the Pre Trial Chamber III decided that a collective approach to victims' application should be encouraged.[205]

The same determination process was adopted by the Pre Trial Chamber in applications in Kenya; then in applications in Central African Republic. The Chamber decided that "the substantive and procedural framework for the possible participation of victims in proceedings at the situation stage set forth in its decision on victims participation in proceedings related to the situation in the Republic of Kenya.[206]

---

[204]Bosco Ntaganda, Trial Chamber, Decision on victims' participation in trial proceedings, 06.02.2015 para 27

[205]Laurent Gbagbo, PTC III, Decision on issues related to the victims' application process, 06 .02. 2012, para 7

[206]Pre-Trial Chamber II, Decision on Victims' Participation in Proceedings Related to the

However, as matter of law, the collective approach cannot be imposed on any victim, thus making it challenging in the event that a single applicant who might be unwilling to join others might proceed, particularly if they cannot afford their own legal representation.

Indeed, Rule 90(1) of the Rules stipulates that a victim shall be free to choose a legal representative; the same rule in its sub-rule 2 provides that:

> Where there are a number of victims, the Chamber may, for the purposes of ensuring the effectiveness of the proceedings, request the victims or particular groups of victims, if necessary with the assistance of the Registry, to choose a common legal representative or representatives...

This can be illustrated by the William Ruto case where some applicants were not satisfied by the Registrar's appointment of legal representative; however their request was ruled against when the Chamber ruled that the appointment had been made rather Regulation 80 of the Regulations which excludes any review against such procedure.[207]

Situation in the Central African Republic, Situation in the Central African republic, 11 November 2010, p 4

[207]Redress. 2012. The participation of victims in international Criminal Court Proceedings, A Review of the Practice and Consideration of Options for the Future. p 56

4

VICTIMS' PARTICIPATION AT THE TRIAL

Art. 68(3) of the Statute and Rule 89(1) of the Rules grant to the Trial Chamber all the powers to authorise participation of victims at the discretion of the Chamber. The process starts with the victim's application for participation which is submitted to the Registrar who shall thereafter transmit the same to the Trial Chamber.

Further the Registrar forwards a copy of the said application to the prosecution and the defence, who are in turn entitled to inform the Chamber on any objection they might have against any particular application.

Though, in the Ntaganda case the Trial Chamber said that "the parties' right to reply to victim applications set out in Rule 89(1) of the Rules is not absolute."[208] Generally, after the Chamber has received the submission from the registry and comment from parties, it makes a determination on the status of applicants and specifies the proceedings and manner in which victims will participate.[209]

At this stage applicants should demonstrate that they meet the requirements of Rule 85 of the Rules which defines the concept of victims, that if they are a natural person, they should prove that they have suffered harm as a result of the commission of the crime, the subject of the proceedings. Alternatively if the victim is an organization Rule 85(b) applies.

[208]Bosco Ntaganda, Trial Chamber, Decision on victims' participation in trial proceedings, 06.02.2015 para 29

[209]Rule 89(1) of the Rules

1. Natural Person

The jurisprudence of the ICC proves how lenient the Court has been as far as the question of proof of identity of a natural person is concerned. For instance in the Gbagbo case[210] the Trial Chamber held that passport; birth certificate; national identity card; driving licence; electoral card; marriage certificate; consular identity card; death certificate; document pertaining to medical treatment, rehabilitation or education; church membership card; family registration booklet; employee identity card; political party membership card; pension booklet; or a signed declaration from two witnesses accompanied by their proof of identity, attesting the identity of the applicant amongst other documents could be accepted as proof of the identity of a natural parson.

The same flexibility is found in the Ntaganda case where the Trial Chmaber equally recognised difficulties that applicants may often have in obtaining or producing copies of official identity documents in the Democratic Republic of Congo.[211] Thus the Chamber further adopted a certain flexibility stating that possible discrepancies between the application and identity documents submitted, if such minor discrepancies do not call into question the overall credibility of the information provided by the applicants, may be accepted,[212] particularly considering record keeping challenges that applicants might have passed through during times of war and the like.

The same Chamber held further that pursuant to rule 85(b) of the Rules, organisations or institutions applying for victim status must establish „direct harm to any of its property which is dedicated to religion, education, art or science or charitable purposes, and to their historic monuments, hospitals and other places and objects for humanitarian purposes."[213]

As explained by Elisabeth Baumgartner, the expansion of the concept of victims is based on the idea that legal entities are often the target of certain war crimes;[214] however organisations and other institutions have not been so far been granted the status of victims within the meaning of this rule, more development will only be expected in the jurisprudence when such status is granted to legal persons.

[210]Laurent Gbagbo, Trial Chamber, Decision on Victims' Participation, 06.03.2015, para 31.

[211]Bosco Ntaganda, Trial Chamber, Decision on victims' participation in trial proceedings, 06.02.2015 para 45

[212]Idem, para 46

[213]Idem, para 51

[214]Elisabeth Baumgartner. 2008. Aspects of victim participation in the proceedings of the International Criminal Court. *90 International Review of the Red Cross 870.* p 420

2. The Concept of Harm

In the Thomas Lubanga case, the Appeals Chamber clarified that the concept of harm should be understood in its ordinary meaning which is hurt, injury and damage, loss which carries the same meaning in legal texts.[215]

This interpretation resonates the same as the Basic Principles and Guidelines on the Right to a Remedy and Reparation for Victims of Gross Violations of International Human Rights Law and Serious Violations of International Humanitarian Law in its principle 8 which defines the concept of victims as persons who individually or collectively suffered harm, including physical or mental injury, emotional suffering, economic loss or substantial impairment of their fundamental rights...[216]

Thus, the Appeals Chamber in the Joseph Kony at al case understood emotional harm to mean any form of psychological harm as expressed in French as *préjudice moral* which it equally understood as mental harm.[217] The same was held by the Appeals Chamber in the Thomas Lubanga case saying that the concept of harm could be material, physical, and psychological which are all forms of harm that fall within the rule if they are suffered personally by the victim.[218]

Furthermore, the harm can be suffered directly or indirectly. As it was held in the Bosco Ntaganda case citing the authority of the Appeals Chamber in the Thomas Lubanga case the harm suffered directly by one victim as a result of the commission of a crime within the jurisdiction of the Court can give rise to harm suffered indirectly by other victims.[219] This could be the case of a family member who suffers psychological harm following a loss of a family member.[220]

---

215 Thomas Lubanga Dyilo, Appeals Chamber, Judgment on the appeals of The Prosecutor and The Defence against Trial Chamber I's Decision on Victims' Participation of 18 January 2008, para 31

216 These Principles and Guidelines were adopted by General Assembly Resolution 60/147 of 16.12.2005

217 Joseph Kony et al., Judgment on the appeals of the Defence against the decisions entitled „Decision on victims' applications for participation a/0010/06, a/0064/06 to a/0070/06, a/0081/06, a/0082/06, a/0084/06 to a/0089/06, a/0091/06 to a/0097/06, a/0099/06, a/0100/06, a/0102/06 to a/0104/06, a/0111/06, a/0113/06 to a/0117/06, a/0120/06, a/0121/06 and a/0123/06 to a/0127/06" of Pre-Trial Chamber II, 23.02. 2009, para 34

218 Thomas Lubanga Dyilo, Appeals Chamber, Judgment on the Appeals of The Prosecutor and The Defence against Trial Chamber I's Decision on Victims' Participation of 18 January 2008, para 32

219 Bosco Ntaganda, Trial Chamber VI, Decision on victims' Participation in Trial Proceedings , para 47

220 For more details see Thomas Lubanga Dyilo, Appeals Chamber, Judgment on the Appeals against

3. The Crime Object of the Proceedings

The presumption of innocence remains a key principle in criminal law. Thus the requirement that victims will be granted such status if the harm they suffered resulted from the crime for which the accused is prosecuted for should not be understood as an implicit determination of the criminal responsibility of the accused. As said by Trial Chamber in the Laurent Gbagbo case, this is a prima facie determination for which it is sufficient that the alleged crimes could have objectively contributed to the harm suffered.[221]

Such a low threshold requirement in the standard of causation requires a proximate cause for the Trial Chamber to grant the status of victim for the purpose of participation to the proceedings; at the end of which proceedings, guilt will be established but the mere participation of a victim is not a verdict in itself, hence the low threshold requirement.

It should be stressed that as demonstrated earlier, nothing prevents the Pre Trial Chamber from allowing victims to participate to its proceedings even at situation phases, in which case no victims can be required to establish the nexus between the harm and the crime charged. For the purposes of participating to the proceedings at the trial phase, charges having been confirmed, the victim will be required to establish the nexus between the harm they allegedly suffered and at least one crime for which the accused is prosecuted.

Obviously after having satisfied the first set of requirements as per Rule 85 of the Rules, the second set of criteria to be satisfied by a victim is provided by Art. 68(3) of the Statute according to which a victim must first and foremost demonstrate how their personal interest is affected by the proceedings.

4. Personal Interest

If a victim wants to prove how their personal interests are affected at a given stage of the trial, they must first satisfy the nexus requirement between the harm they suffered and at least one of the crimes charged against the accused. Then they must demonstrate how a given issue which is to be decided by the Trial Chamber will affect them directly.

---

the "Decision establishing the principles and procedures to be applied to reparations" of 7 August 2012 with amended order for reparations (Annex A) and Public Annexes 1 and 2, para191

[221]Laurent Gbagbo, Decision on Victim Participation, 6.03.2015, para, 36

Thus as held by the Trial Chamber in the Jean Pierre Bemba case a general interest in the punishment of the criminals to uphold criminal principal cannot suffice as to meet the required threshold for the purposes of proving personal interest.[222] Whereas in the Germain Katanga case, the Trail Chamber II considered that all victims who suffered from the crime committed within the geographical and temporal limit of the crime charged, had personal interest before the Chamber.[223]

The Trial Chamber II was of the view that legitimate interest of victims may be invoked when seeking to establish facts subject to the proceedings. Victims' views may help the Chamber to understand what really happened; however a decision on the submission of such views can only be taken on a case by case basis in consideration of facts at hand.

5. Modality of Participation

The recognition of the status of victim by the Trial Chamber gives such victims a range of rights, subject to the modality determined by the relevant chamber. Indeed, the Rules contain provisions on such participation including participation through attendance at the hearing, receiving notification, accessing records, filing responses, making oral submission and the possibility of presenting evidence amongst others.

5.1. Participation through Attendance to Hearings

Rule 91 (2) of the Rules provides that: „A legal representative of a victim shall be entitled to attend and participate in the proceedings in accordance with the terms of the ruling of the Chamber and any modification thereof given under Rules 89 and 90. This shall include participation in hearings unless, in the circumstances of the case, the Chamber concerned is of the view that the representative's intervention should be confined to written observations or submissions."

[222]Jean Pierre Bemba, Trial Chamber III, Corrigendum to Decision on the participation of victims in the trial and on 86 applications by victims to participate in the proceedings, 12.07.2010 para 25
[223]Germain Katanga and Mathieu Ngudjolo Chui, Trial Chamber II, Urgent Decision on the Modalities of Victim Participation at Trial, 22.01.2010, para 61

Once a victim's status has been determined, their attendance to the court proceedings has never been contested. However as to proceedings before the Pre Trial Chamber, if the circumstances of the case are such that hearings are not public, it will be upon the Trial Chamber to decide on the modalities of victims' participation.

5.2. Right to receive Notifications

Rule 92 (5) of the Rules provides that:

> In a manner consistent with the ruling made under rules 89 to 91, victims or their legal representatives participating in proceedings shall, in respect of those proceedings, be notified by the Registrar in a timely manner of:
> (a) Proceedings before the Court, including the date of hearings and any postponements thereof, and the date of delivery of the decision;
> (b) Requests, submissions, motions and other documents relating to such requests, submissions or motions.

The practice of the Court has been that whenever filings are done the filing party indicates which other parties might be interested in such filing, including as the case may be which particular victim might be interested for the purposes of facilitating their notifications.

5.3. Right to access Court Records

Rule 131 (2) of the Rules provides that:

> Subject to any restrictions concerning confidentiality and the protection of national security information, the record may be consulted by the Prosecutor, the defence, the representatives of States when they participate in the proceedings, and the victims or their legal representatives participating in the proceedings pursuant to rules 89 to 91.

In the Jean Pierre Bemba case, the Trial Chamber III held that: "[I]n order to facilitate full participation by victims, it is in the interests of justice that those who have been granted leave to participate are afforded access to the confidential material in the case, relevant to their views and concerns."[224]

It should however be indicated that the access to confidential materials is not unlimited. In the event that such materials contain information that could compromise the security of any other individual or any such information cannot be availed to victims even when they are part of the Court's record. The same would apply if the confidential materials are subject of a protective measure concealing some information which could have the same effects.

It is in that respect that Trial Chamber I in the Thomas Lubanga case held that participating victims have the right to consult the record of the proceedings, including the index, subject to any restrictions concerning confidentiality and the protection of national security information.[225]

5.4. Right to make Oral Submissions

Generally various Trial Chambers have allowed victims to make opening and closing remarks under the provisions of Rule 89(1) of the Rules[226] according to which:

> In order to present their views and concerns, victims shall make written application to the Registrar, who shall transmit the application to the relevant Chamber [...] the Chamber shall then specify the proceedings and manner in which participation is considered appropriate, which may include making opening and closing statements.

The Prosecution and the defence are nevertheless entitled to respond to victims submissions.

---

[224]Jean Pierre Bemba Gombo, Trial Chamber III, Corrigendum to Decision on the participation of victims in the trial and on 86 applications by victims to participate in the proceedings, 12.07. 2010 para 47

[225]Thomas Lubanga Dyilo, Trial Chamber I, Decision on victims' participation, 18.10. 2008, para 105

[226]Gideon Boas et al., International Criminal Procedure: International Criminal Law Practioner Library Series Vol. III, Cambridge University Press, 2011, pp 316-317

5.5. Right to question Witnesses

Rule 91(3) (a) of the Rules provides for the procedure applicable to a legal representative of victims who is attending and participating to the proceedings when they wish to question witnesses. It states that: „When a legal representative attends and participates in accordance with this rule, and wishes to question a witness, including questioning under rules 67 and 68, an expert or the accused, the legal representative must make application to the Chamber."

After having received such application, the Chamber issues a ruling on the same taking into consideration the rights of the accused, the interests of witnesses, the need for a fair, impartial and expeditious trial and in order to give effect to article 68, paragraph 3.[227]

Thus Trial Chamber III in the Jean Pierre Bemba Gombo, citing the Authority of Trial Chamber II in the Germain Katanga case which recognised that the legal representatives of victims may question witnesses, including experts or the accused. [228] The Trial Chamber III affirmed that such intervention could enable the Chamber to understand some of the matters at issue, given the victims' knowledge of social and cultural background.[229]

5.6. Right to present Evidence

There is no *expressis verbis* provision for victims to tender evidence to the Court. However the Court has constructively interpreted various provisions of the Statute and the Rules to that effect. Indeed considering that the intervention of victims, is mainly left to the discretion of the concerned chamber, the jurisprudence of the Court has allowed the submission of evidence under Art. 69(3) is fine according to which the Court shall have the authority to request the submission of all evidence that it considers necessary for the determination of the truth.

Thus in the Germain Katanga and Mathieu Ngudjolo Chui cases, the Trial Chamber II stressed that such participation was only a possibility afforded to

[227]Rule 91(3) (b) of the Rules

[228]Jean Pierre Bemba Gombo, Trial Chamber III, Corrigendum to Decision on the Participation of Victims in the Trial and on 86 Applications by Victims to Participate in the Proceedings, 12.07. 2010 para 33

[229]Idem

the victims in order to give effect to the provisions of article 68(3) of the Statute, once the victims' interests, the rights of the accused and the requirements of a fair and impartial trial have been duly balanced.[230]

In the William Ruto case, after having noted that other chambers have acknowledged that victims may possess evidence that may assist the Chamber in its determination of the truth in accordance with Article 69(3) of the Statute, the Trial Chamber V indicated that "the Common Legal Representative may submit a discreet application for the presentation of evidence, After having granted the parties an opportunity to provide their observations on such requests, the Chamber will then determine, pursuant to Articles 64(6)(d) and 69(3) of the Statute, whether the proposed evidence is relevant to the personal interests of victims, if it may contribute to the determination of the truth and whether it would be consistent with the rights of the accused and a fair and impartial trial."[231]

5.7. Interlocutory Appeals

As a matter of law, the right of appeal against any court decision belongs exclusively to either party to the proceedings. In theory, this seems to lock out victims from any possibility to initiate any appeals to any decision save for reparation orders.

However in the event that one party to the proceedings has been granted leave to appeal, any victim who will demonstrate that their rights are affected by the concerned decision can be granted right to participate to the interlocutory appeals. Thus such participation is only dependant on a possibility of an appeal initiated by either the prosecution or the defence and never by victims themselves.

5.8. Victims Witness Dual Status

In the event that a given victim whose status has already been affirmed by the Chamber is called upon by a party to the proceedings as a witness, such victim will appear before the Court as a witness without losing their victim's

[230]Germain Katanga and Mathieu Ngudjolo Chui , Urgent Decision on the Modalities of Victim Participation at Trial, 22.01.2010, para 83

[231]William Ruto and Joshua Arap Sang, Decision on Victims' Representation and Participation, Trial Chamber V, 03.10.2012 para 77

status hence the dual victim witness status. In the Thomas Lubanga case the Trial Chamber I rejected the submission of the defence that victims appearing before the Court should be treated automatically as witnesses hence losing their victim status.[232]

However the Trial Chamber held that when considering the modalities of participation by victims with dual status, there will be need to strike a correct balance between the victims' participation and the rights of the defence including the right of the accused to a fair and expeditious trial.[233]

When a victim is sworn in as a witness they are guided by the same regulations relevant to other witnesses. That is, they make a solemn undertaking that they will speak the truth, the whole truth and nothing but the truth, as provided for by Rule 66 of the Rules. The Rules are further explained, that as provided by Art. 70 of the Statute the Court shall jurisdiction over them should they give false testimony which is an crime against the administration of justice.

Contrary to other submissions they might have made as victim, submissions which is not made under oath, which is neither cross-examined evidence given by victims in their status of witness fail to meet the requirements of Art. 74(2) which requires the Court to base its decision only on evidence submitted and discussed before it at the trial.

[232]Thomas Lubanga Dyilo, Trial Chamber I, Decision on Victims' Participation, 18. 01. 2008, para 132

[233]Idem, para 134

5

THE ICC VICTIMS' REPARATION REGIME

The Max Planck Encyclopedia of Public International Law defines the concept of reparation to mean a "recompense given to one who has suffered legal injury at the hands of another; to make amends, provide restitution, or give satisfaction or compensation for a wrong inflicted."[234]

In its historical background, the concept of reparation can be traced in the history of the World Wars. Indeed, the 1919 Treaty of Peace between the Allied and Associated Powers and Germany, the Versailles Peace Treaty contained provisions on reparation.

As the WWI the reparations were mainly considered war indemnities, such indemnities were to be paid by the vanquished nations to the victorious nations and were generally considered as compensations for the cost of the war. One of the novelties of the WWII reparation system would be that such reparation was extended to individual compensations given to Holocaust survivors,[235] thus the appearance of individual reparations in international practices.

Reparation is considered part of restorative justice,[236] which itself is part of transitional justice system. In international law, transitional justice "is concerned with the question how to confront a situation of past large-scale human rights violations and humanitarian abuses in a period of transition to peace and democracy."[237]

---

[234]Dinah Shelton, Reparation, in Max- Planck Encyclopedia of Public International Law

[235]Garcia-Godos. 2008. Victim Reparations in Transitional Justice – What it takes and Why. In *Nordisk Tidsskrift for for Menneskerettigheter 26*. p 119

[236]Idem, p 120

[237]Anja Seibert-Fohr, Transitional Justice in Post-Conflict Situations in Max – Planck Encyclopedia of Public International Law

Within the ICC legal regime, Art 75 of the Statute and Rule 98 of Rules contain relevant provisions to victims, accordingly:
Art 75 states that:

1. The Court shall establish principles relating to reparations to, or in respect of, victims, including restitution, compensation and rehabilitation. On this basis, in its decision the Court may, either upon request or on its own motion in exceptional circumstances, determine the scope and extent of any damage, loss and injury to, or in respect of, victims and will state the principles on which it is acting.
2. The Court may make an order directly against a convicted person specifying appropriate reparations to, or in respect of, victims, including restitution, compensation and rehabilitation. Where appropriate, the Court may order that the award for reparations be made through the Trust Fund provided for in article 79.
3. Before making an order under this article, the Court may invite and shall take account of representations from or on behalf of the convicted person, victims, other interested persons or interested States.
4. In exercising its power under this article, the Court may, after a person is convicted of a crime within the jurisdiction of the Court, determine whether, in order to give effect to an order which it may make under this article, it is necessary to seek measures under article 93, paragraph 1.
5. A State Party shall give effect to a decision under this article as if the provisions of article 109 were applicable to this article.
6. Nothing in this article shall be interpreted as prejudicing the rights of victims under national or international law.

Rule 98 of the Rules states that:

1. Individual awards for reparations shall be made directly against a convicted person.
2. The Court may order that an award for reparations against a convicted person be deposited with the Trust Fund where at the time of making the order it is impossible or impracticable to make individual awards directly to each victim. The award for

reparations thus deposited in the Trust Fund shall be separated from other resources of the Trust Fund and shall be forwarded to each victim as soon as possible.

3. The Court may order that an award for reparations against a convicted person be made through the Trust Fund where the number of the victims and the scope, forms and modalities of reparations makes a collective award more appropriate.
4. Following consultations with interested States and the Trust Fund, the Court may order that an award for reparations be made through the Trust Fund to an intergovernmental, international or national organization approved by the Trust Fund.
5. Other resources of the Trust Fund may be used for the benefit of victims subject to the provisions of article 79.

Thus in its first decision on reparation the Trial Chamber I recognized that the Statute and the Rules introduce a system of reparations that recognizes the need to go beyond the notion of punitive justice, towards a solution which is more inclusive, encourages participation and recognises the need to provide effective remedies for victims.[238]

1. Eligibility Criteria

In its judgment on the appeals against the "decision establishing the principles and procedures to be applied to reparations" of 7 August 2012, the Appeals' Chamber indicated that an order for reparation must amongst other factors determine who is eligible for reparation under Art. 75 of the Statute.

Regulation 46 of the Regulations stipulates that: "Resources collected through awards for reparations may only benefit victims as defined in Rule 85 of the Rules of Procedure and Evidence, and, where natural persons are concerned, their families, affected directly or indirectly by the crimes committed by the convicted person."

It should not be surprising that the eligibility is re-discussed at this point considering that for the purposes of reparations, the concept of victim includes

[238]Thomas Lubanga, Trial Chamber I, Decision Establishing the Principles and Procedures to be applied to Reparations, para 177

victims who participated in the trial and those who applied for reparations even though they might not have participated to earlier proceedings.[239]

Furthermore, with regard to reparations, the Court has been consistent recognising that all victims are to be treated fairly and equally irrespective of whether they participated in the trial proceedings, as it has recognized that direct as well indirect victims meet the eligibility criteria.[240]

Thus, Rule 94(1) of the Rules prescribes that a victim's application for reparations under Art. 75 shall contain the following particulars:

> (a) The identity and address of the claimant;
> (b) A description of the injury, loss or harm;
> (c) The location and date of the incident and, to the extent possible, the identity of the person or persons the victim believes to be responsible for the injury, loss or harm;
> (d) Where restitution of assets, property or other tangible items is sought, a description of them;
> (e) Claims for compensation;
> (f) Claims for rehabilitation and other forms of remedy;
> (g) To the extent possible, any relevant supporting documentation, including names and addresses of witnesses.

It is commendable that the practice of the Court has been that as far as applicant seeking reparation is concerned, the standard of proof of their identity and the harm they allegedly suffered has been lowered to a balance of probabilities. This means that a given applicant is only required to show that it is more probable than not that they have suffered harm caused by at least one crime for which the conviction has been done.[241]

Many factors could justify the lowering of such a standard of proof. Indeed the environment in which such crimes are committed makes it hard for victims to keep track of all official records hence the reason why the Court has usually accepted official documents as well as unofficial documents[242] and in some instances testimony of witnesses in lieu of some documentations.

The fact that it takes generally more than a decade between the time a given

---

[239] Thomas Lubanga, Trial Chamber I, Decision on Reparations, para 187

[240] Idem

[241] Germain Katanga, Trial Chamber II, Order for Reparations pursuant to Article 75 of the Statute, para 50

[242] Idem, para 71

crime is committed and the time the reparation order is issued in the context of nearly break down of the State machinery, it would not be realistic for the Court to keep any high standard of proof such as beyond any reasonable doubt.

It is in that vein that in the Al Mahdi case, the Chamber adopted a flexible approach and accepted distinct forms of identification. The Chamber further stated that it also believed it was necessary to extend such flexibility to possible discrepancies between the application and identity documents submitted. Hence, minor discrepancies which do not call into question the overall credibility of the information provided by the applicant, were accepted. [243]

One may additionally submit that much the accepting of an application for the purpose of reparations remains part of the ICC judicial proceedings, as per the ICC legal structure. Such determination is not necessarily part of the criminal proceedings which would otherwise require a higher standard of proof.

2. Nexus to the Crime for which the Conviction is based

In the Thomas Lubanga case, the Appeals Chamber held that the reparation order "must identify the victim's eligibility to benefit from the awards for reparations or set out the criteria of eligibility based on the link between the harm suffered by the victims and the crimes for which the person was convicted." [244]

This position had been previously stated by the Trial Chamber I as it found that "The "damage, loss and injury," which form the basis of a reparations claim, must have resulted from the crimes of enlisting and conscripting children under the age of 15 and using them to participate actively in the hostilities."[245]

However the Trial Chamber II in the Germain Katanga case brought in a certain nuance saying that the Chamber does not regard itself as in a position to determine that the physical and psychological harm occasioned by rape and/or sexual violence or gender-based violence during the attack on Bogoro ensued from one of the crimes of which Mr Katanga was convicted.[246]

---

[243] Al Mahdi, Trial Chamber VIII, Public redacted version of 'Decision on Victim Participation at Trial and on Common Legal Representation of Victims', para 18-19

[244] Appeals Chamber, Judgment on the Appeals Against the "Decision Establishing the Principles and Procedures to be Applied to Reparations" of 7 August 2012 with AMENDED order for reparations (Annex A) and public annexes 1 and 2, para 1

[245] Thomas Lubanga, Trial Chamber I, Decision Establishing the Principles and Procedures to be applied to Reparations, para 247

[246] Idem, para 152

Though the Chamber found that applicants who alleged that they suffered physical and psychological harm occasioned by rape, sexual violence or gender-based violence, crimes which were not charged against the convicted person, such „victims" have also sought reparations for other harms resulting from the attack on Bogoro. Although the Chamber has found that they had equally suffered other harm,[247] it nevertheless still invited the Trust Fund to afford consideration as part of its assistance mandate, wherever possible, to these applicants[248]

In another instance, the Chamber held that it was unable to infer a direct nexus to suggest that the Accused used these children to participate in the hostilities,[249] as Mr Katanga had already been acquitted for the same: thus the Chamber concluded that the former child soldiers were ineligible for reparations in the present proceedings brought in connection with the crimes of which Mr Katanga was convicted.

The Chamber had again invited the TFV to give consideration as part of its assistance mandate, wherever possible, to the harm suffered by the applicants in the attack on Bogoro upon which the Chamber had not been in a position to act in the case.[250]

3. Types of Reparations

Rule 97 (1) of the Rules provides that: "Taking into account the scope and extent of any damage, loss or injury, the Court may award reparations on an individualised basis or, where it deems it appropriate, on a collective basis or both."

Whereas Rule 98(3) of the Rules says: "The Court may order that an award for reparations against a convicted person be made through the Trust Fund where the number of the victims and the scope, forms and modalities of reparations makes a collective award more appropriate."

Thus in the Germain Katanga case, the Trial Chamber II defined individual reparation as such reparation where the ensuing benefit is afforded directly to an individual to repair the harm he or she suffered as a consequence of crimes

[247]Idem, para 153

[248]Idem, para 154

[249]Idem, para 160

[250]Idem, para 161

of which the person was convicted. The same Chamber considers collective reparation such reparations given to group or category of person who share identity or experience to benefit them as a group.[251]

Furthermore, it should be noted that the issue of an order of individual reparation does not exclude collective reparation or vice verse, as such orders can be given concurrently.

4. The Trust Fund for Victims

Adopted through the Resolution ICC-ASP/I/1/Res.6 of 09.09.2002, the trust fund for the benefit of victims of crimes within the jurisdiction of the Court, and families of such victims is funded primarily by voluntary contribution from governments, international organisations, corporations and through monies collected through fine or forfeiture transferred by the Court order.[252]

One may submit that the creation of the Trust Fund is the most creative idea as far as the restorative mandate of the ICC is concerned. However, as far the ICC proceedings are concerned, the Trust Fund for Victims should not be confused with the *partie civilement responsible* mainly familiar to civil law systems.

Thus in the Thomas Lubanga case the Appeals Chamber held that the Trial Chamber must still direct the order "against" the convicted person even when such reparations are ordered "through" the Trust Fund in accordance with the second sentence of article 75 (2) of the Statute.[253]

Such stand was prompted by the earlier decision of the Trial Chamber I which has ambiguously decided that considering that the convicted person has been declared indigent, Mr Lubanga was only able to contribute to non-monetary reparations, thus limiting his responsibility to symbolic reparation including an apology to the victims, subject to his agreement,[254] thus issuing the reparation order through the Trust Fund without mentioning Mr. Lubanga's responsibility.[255]

---

[251]Germain Katanga, Trial Chamber II, Order for Reparations pursuant to Article 75 of the Statute, para 273-274

[252]Resolution ICC-ASP/I/1/Res.6 of 09.09.2002

[253]Thoma Lubanga, Appeals Chamber, Judgment on the Appeals Against the "Decision Establishing the Principles and Procedures to be Applied to Reparations" of 7 August 2012 with Amended order for Reparations (Annex A) and Public Annexes 1 and 2, Para 70

[254] Idem Para 269

[255] Idem Para 270

Nevertheless the jurisprudence of the Court seems settled as it has made all subsequent reparation orders against the convicted irrespective of their financial ability. Such position may be supported by Regulation 50(b) of the Regulations according to which: "When the Court makes an order for reparations against a convicted person and orders that the award be deposited with or made through the Trust Fund in accordance with rule 98, sub-rules 2 to 4 of the Rules of Procedure and Evidence."[256]

[256]The same interpretation is found in the Appeals Chamber decision in the Thomas Lubanga, Appeals Chamber, Judgment on the Appeals against the "Decision establishing the Principles and Procedures to be Applied to Reparations" of 7 August 2012 with amended order for reparations (Annex A) and public annexes 1 and 2, at para 73

CONCLUDING REMARKS

The objective of this study has been double folded as it is aimed at analysing how the participation of victims to the ICC proceedings and its reparation mechanism work for the purposes of evaluating their contribution to the achievement of the ICC restorative role.

1. Victims' Participation

It is noticeable that the process of eligibility for the status of victim can be relatively long and cumbersome. This might be explained by the fact that the number of victims which has inevitably continued to grow when resources either in terms of finances or manpower cannot march the number of victims. Obviously such hurdles have resulted in to a number of frustrations for victims and their representatives at times even other staff of the Court.

However this alone cannot constitute a measuring tool to assess the efficiency of the process, one might consider checking whether such trouble will be rewarded by an equivalent outcome to arrive at a conclusion on the way forward.

At the outmost it needs to be indicated that finding the way forward to such a controversial question might go beyond this research. Such a result is attained after inclusive consultations with various stake holders, in various forums. Indeed it is rather the purpose of this research to stimulate the debate and invite various parties to rethink any possible improvement. Nevertheless there are a concerns which could be considered as starting points for the debate.

By way of literal interpretation, the very concept of participation to the proceedings would mean taking part to such proceedings. According to the current regime, victims are not per se parties to the proceedings, but the spirit of the ICC legal regime is that such regime affords them some participatory rights.

Such participatory rights enable them the possibility to appear in court and to be heard by the Court, or at least that is the spirit which prompted the drafters of the Rome Statute if at all the concept of participation is to be given its meaning. However, practice shows that such possibility of a given victim to appear before the Court is a rather remote dream irrespective of the existence of legal provision to that effect.

Victims' participation has rather been restricted to the possibilities offered to their respective counsel to make their legal representations. The general practice is that the legal representation does not exclude the right of the concerned person to equally appear in person even when assisted by their counsel which isn't the case with victims whose legal representation is automatically considered as their replacement.

Perhaps more strikingly, whether victims would appear in person or will express their views exclusively through their legal representation, one is left with one pertinent question as to what are the value of such views expressed?

The above question begs for an answer considering that the current fashion of victims' participation does not meet the requirement of Art. 74(2) and thus are not considered as part of evidence upon which the Court may base its decision. Indeed, victims views are not given under oath as victims are not subjected to any cross-examination process and thus excluded from the Court's evidence.

If when making their determinations, judges do not decide based on viticms submissions, what then will be the purposes of going through such a process demanding process to victims, a process which is equally costly to the Court when a victim status brings so little to the process?

On the one hand, if the question of the threshold of victims' submissions for the purposes of the Court's consideration is cured by the possibility of a witness appearing in court as a witness, as already discussed, one may still be tempted to call for an amendment of the relevant legal provisions to redesign such participation to include a different method which shall enable the Court to consider a victim's deposition as part of the Court evidence not only in cases where they appear in court with a witness-victim double status.

It might be worth considering a possibility of raising the status of victims a notch high and affording them full participatory rights modelled on *partie civile* familiar with the civil law jurisdictions. However for the purposes of making the system more efficient, considering the need to respect the rights of the accused person which constitutes their basic rights, such status might be limited to victims who are ready to take the solemn oath and who accept to be cross-examined and who understand that would they give false evidence to the Court they would become subject to criminal proceedings for pervert the course of justice. Furthermore, the Chamber would have the discretion to grant such status to any victim it deems appropriate according to the relevance of submissions they intend to make.

On the other hand, in the search for an answer to the purposes of the victims' participation in the criminal proceedings, the answer might be that the intervention of victim is considered as part their healing process and serve as reconciliatory purposes as demonstrated by relevant theories of restorative justice. A follow up question becomes nevertheless whether criminal proceedings could be the most appropriate forum for such purpose.

There is no doubt about the intention of the drafters of the Rome Statute to create a Court which at the same time deliver retributive justice and equally affords restorative justice to victims. It remains however a question at to how such combination is done. A close look at the ICC reparation system might provide answers to such questions.

2. Victim's Reparation

As indicated earlier, it is encouraging to note how the Court has lowered the standard of proof for the purposes of reparations to the "balance of probability." Such acceptable standard prevents victims from going through a frustrating process which as we have seen has ended up adding salt to the victims' wounds.

Thus flexibility that has characterised the Court with regard how the reparation process can be taken forward for consideration given to the vulnerability of victim and constitute part of their healing process particularly those affected psychologically.

Secondly victims' participation to the reparation process is another area which gives an opportunity for victims to appear before the Court and tell their story. This cannot be considered as shifting the load from the trial process to the reparation mechanism since these two are not applying the same standard, do not have the same flexibility and, *stricto sensu* their focus is designed differently.

Whereas criminal proceedings should retain a focus on their primary mission, which is establishing guilt, the reparation mechanism should be victim centered. Indeed, one may be tempted to advocate for a reparation system which is less judicial even when such mechanism might remain within ICC auspices; the mechanism would rather be more restorative thus leaning more towards mechanisms available under transitional justice.

SELECTED BIBLIOGRAPHY

1. Books and Journal Articles

Abdreas O' Shea. 2011. Truth and Reconciliation Commissions. In *Max-Planck Encyclopedia of Public International Law*

Alexander L. Boraine. 2006. Transitional Justice: A Holistic Interpretation, *60 Journal of International Affaire1*

Anja Seibert-Fohr, Transitional Justice in Post-Conflict Situations in Max – Planck Encyclopedia of Public International Law

Antonio Cassese. 2008. *International Criminal Law*, Second Edition, Oxford University Press

Anuradha Saibaba Rajesh. 2009. Victims in the International Criminal Court: Vindicated or Vanquished. *9 ISIL Y.B. Int'l Human. & Refugee L. 120*

Bridie McAsey. 2010. Victim Participation at the International Criminal Court and its Impact on Procedural Fairness, *Australian International Law Journal*

Carla Ferstman. 2002. The Reparation Regime of the International Criminal Court: Practical Consideration. In *Leiden Journal of International Law*

Carsten Stahn. Héctor Olásolo. Kate Gibson. 2006. Participation of Victims in Pre-Trial Proceedings of the ICC. In *Journal of International Criminal Justice 4*

Charles Barton. 2000. Empowerment and Retribution in Criminal Justice. In *Restorative Justice, Philosophy to Practice.* Ashgate

Charles P. Trumbull. 2008. The Victims of Victim Participation in International Criminal Proceedings, *Michigan Journal of international law 29*

Christine H. Chung. 2008. Victims' Participation at the International Criminal Court: Are Concessions of the Court Clouding the Promise? In *6 Northwestern Journal of International Human Rights 3*

Christine Van den Wyngaert.2011. Victims before International Criminal Courts: Some Views and Concerns of an ICC Trial Judge. *44 Case W. Res. J. Int'l L. 475*

D.D. Rishi. 1998. Victim and Punishment of the Offender. In *Human Rights and Victimology.* cited by Timothy K. Kuhner

di Giuseppe Zago. 2014. The Role of Victims at the International Criminal Court: Legal Challenges from the Tension between Restorative and Retributive Justice. in *Diritto Penale Contemporaneo*

Dzhangir Kerimov. 1989. *Methology of Law*. Progress Publishers

Edgar Bodenheimer.1962. *Jurisprudence: The Philosophy and Method of the Law.* Harvard University Press.

Elisabeth Baumgartner. 2008. Aspects of victim participation in the proceedings of the International Criminal Court, *90 International Review of the Red Cross 870*

Ellen A. Waldman. 2003. Healing Hearts or Righting Wrongs?: A Meditation on the Goals of Restorative Justice, in *25 Hamline Journal of Public Law & Policy 1*

Elmar G. M. Weitekamp. *The History of Restorative Justice* as cite by Douglas J. Sylvester. 2002. Myth in Restorative Justice History. *2003 Utah Law Review 1*

Emily Haslam and Rod Edmunds.2013. Victim Participation, Politics and the Construction of Victims at the International Criminal Court: Reflections on Proceedings in Banda and Jerbo, *Melbourne Journal of International Law 14*

Emmanuel Vergé Ed. 1969. *Répertoire de Droit Pénal et de Procédure Pénale, „partie civile,“* Tome III. Dalloz

Fernandez de Casadevante Romani. 2010. International Law of Victims, *14 Max Planck Y.B. U.N. L. 219*

Frankfort, et al.1951. *Before Phylosophy*, Pelican. pp 99-100, as cited by R. Neil Snyder. *Natural Law and Equity*, in Ralph A. Newman.1973. *Equity in the world's legal systems, a comparative study*, Etablissements Emile Bruylant

Garcia-Godos. 2008. Victim Reparations in Transitional Justice – What it takes and Why. In *Nordisk Tidsskrift for for Menneskerettigheter 26*

Gideon Boas et al. 2011. *International Criminal Procedure, International Criminal Law Practitioner Library.* Cambridge University Press

Guido Acquaviva. 2008. New Paths in International Criminal Justice? The Internal Rules of the Cambodian Extraordinary Chambers. In *Journal of International Criminal Justice 6*

Hugo Grotious.1995. *De Jure Belli ac Pacis Libri Tres.* Translation Book I by Francis W. Kelsey, William S. Hein

Human Right Watch. 2008. *Courting History, The Landmark International Criminal Court's First Years.*

Ilaria Bottigliero. 2004. *Redress for Victims of Crimes under International Law.* Martinus Nijhoff Publishers

J.E. Alvarez. 1999. Crimes of State/Crimes of Hate: Lessons from Rwanda, in *Yale Journal of International Law*

Janine Natalya Clark. 2009. The Limits of Retributive Justice: Findings of an Empirical Study in Bosnia and Hercegovina. In *Journal of International Criminal Justice 7*

Jean Hampton. 1991. An Expressive Theory of Retribution. In *Retrbutivism and its Critics.* Franz Steiner Veröags Stuttgart

Jeffrie G. Murhpy. 1979. *Retribution Justice and Therapy, Essays in the Philosophy of Law.* Reidel Publishing Company

Jeffrie G. Murphy. 1992. *Retribution Reconsidered: More essays in the philosophy of Law*, Kluwer Academic Publishers.

Jemima Garcia-Godos.2008. Victim Reparations in Transitional Justice, What is at Stake and Why. *26 Nordisk Tidsskrift for Menneskerettigheter 2*

Jeremy Bentham. 1945. *The Limits of Jurisprudence Defined*, Columbia University Press.

Jérome de Hamptinne. 2010. Challenges raised by Victims' Participation in the Proceedings of the Special Tribunal for Lebanon, in *Journal for International Criminal Justice 8*

Jim Consedine. 1999. The Third Millennium - Restorative Justice or more Crime and Prisons? *Sri Lanka Journal of International Law 11*

John Jackson. 2009. Finding the Best Epistemic fit for International Criminal Tribunals, Beyond the Adversarial-Inquisitorial Dichotomy, in *Journal of International Criminal Justice 7*

John L. Ginn. Sugamo Prison. 1992. *Tokyo: An Account of the Trial and Sentencing of Japanese War Criminal in 1948 by a U.S. Participant.* McFarland& Company

John Pritchard. 1998. *The Tokyo Major War Crimes Trials.* The Edwin Mellen Press.

Kader Asmal. 2000. Truth Reconciliation and Justice: the South African Experience in Perspective. *63 The Modern Law Review 1*

Karen Brounéus. Reconciliation and Development. *International Conference Building a Future on Peace and Justice.* Nuremberg, 25-27 June 2007

Kate Gibson and Daniella Rudy. 2009. A New Model of International Criminal Procedure? The Progress of the Duch Trial at the ECCC.In *Journal of International Criminal Justice7*

Kathleen Daly. 2004. Restorative Justice: The Real Story. In *Restorative Justice*, Ashgate Dartmouth

Kelisiana Thynne.2009. The International Criminal Court: A Failure of International Justice for Victims. *46 Alta. L. Rev. 957*

King, F. and La Rosa A. *International Criminal Tribunal for the Former Yugoslavia: Current Survey-the Jurisprudence of the Yugoslavia Tribunal:1994-1996*

Lyn S. Graybill. 2002. *Truth & Reconciliation in South Africa, Miracle or Model?* Lynne Rienner Publishers

M. Akida, Criminal law in Nathalie Bernard-Maugiron and Baudouin Dupret. 2002. *Egypt and its Laws.* Kluwer Law International

Manoj Kumar Sinha. 2003. Are European Inquisitorial and Adversarial Criminal Justice Systems Converging? In *43 Indian Journal of International Law 1*

Mariana Pena. 2010. Victim Participation at the International Criminal Court: Achievements Made and Challenges Lying Ahead. In *16 ILSA Journal of International and Comparative Law 2*

Mark A. Drumbl. 2007. *Atrocity, Punishment, and International Law.* Cambridge University Press

Mark Findlay. 2001. Synthesis in Trial Procedures? The Experience of International Criminal Tribunals, in *50 The International and Comparative Law Quarterly 1*

Mark R. Reiff. 2005. Punishment, Compensation and Law: A Theory of Enforceability. Cambridge University Press

Markus Funk.2015. Surveying the Rise of Victims' Rights under International Law (and at the International Criminal Court). *11 Eyes on the ICC 3*

Matthew Lippman. 1989. Islamic Criminal Law and Procedure: Religious Fundamentalism v. Modern Law, *12 Boston College International and Comparative Law Review 1*

Mauro Politi and Federica Gioia. 2002. *The Criminal Procedure before the International Criminal Court: Main Features,* in The Law and Practice of International Courts and Tribunals

Michael G. Palmer.2004. Compensation for Vietnam's Agent Orange Victims, in *8 International Journal of Human Rights 1*

Patric Olivelle. 2005. *Manu's Code of Law, A Critical Edition and Translation of the Manava-Dharmásatra.* Oxford University Press

Paul Roberts and Nesam McMillan. 2003. For Criminology in International Justice. In *Journal of International Criminal Justice 1*

Research. Hart Publishing

Reza Banakar and Max Travers. 2005. *Law, Sociology and Method, Theory and Method in Socio-Legal*

Robert Campbell. 1885. *Lectures on Jurisprudence or the Philosophy of Positive Law by the Late John Austin.* Fifth Edition. John Murray

Robert Cryer et al. 2010. An Introduction to International Criminal Law and Procedure, Second Edition, Cambridge University Press

Roger P. Alford. 2006. War Reparations, the Holocaust, and the ICC in *Die Nürnberger Prozesse Völkerstrafrecht seit 1945.* K.G. Saur München

Sam Garkawe. 2006. The role and rights of victims at the Nuremberg International Military Tribunal, in *Die Nürnberger Prozesse Völkerstrafrecht seit 1945.* K.G. Saur München

Sheldon Amos. 1881. *The Science of Law, Fifth Edition,* C. Kegan Paul & CO.

Silvia D'Ascoli. 2011. *Sentencing in International Criminal Law, the UN Ad Hoc Tribunals and Future Perspectives for the ICC,* Hart Publishing

Solis Horwitz. 1950. The Toky Trial. In *International Conciliation, Carnegie Endowment for International Peace*

Susan Dimock. 1963. *Classic Readings and Cases in the Philosophy of Law.* Pearson Longman

Theo van Boven. 2009. Victims' Rights and Interest in the International Criminal Court, in *The Legal Regime of the International Criminal Court, Essays in Honour of Professor Igor Blishchenko.* Martinus Nojhoff Publishers

Tony F. Marshall. 1999. *Restorative Justice: An overview.* A report by the Home Office Research Development and Statistics Directorate

Tzvetan Todorov.2009. Memory as Remedy for Evil. In *Journal of International Criminal Justice 7*

Vasselin Popovski.2000. The international Criminal Court: A Synthesis of Retributive and Restorative Justice, in *XV International Relations 3*

William A. Schabas. 2004. *An Introduction to the International Criminal Court.* Second Edition. Cambridge University Press

William A. Schabas. 2007. *An Introduction to the International Criminal Court.* Third Edition. Cambridge University Press

William A. Schabas. 2010. *The International Criminal Court, A commentary on the Rome Statute.* Oxford University Press

Legal and Quasi Legal Sources

1948 Universal Declaration of Human Rights

1950 European Convention for the Protection of Human Rights and Fundamental Freedoms

1965 International Convention on the Elimination of All Forms of Racial Discrimination

1966 International Covenant on Civil and Political Rights

1969 American Convention on Human Rights

1981 African Charter on Human and Peoples' Rights

1983 European Convention on the Compensation of Victims of Violent Crime

1984 Convention against Torture and Other Cruel, Inhuman or Degrading Treatment or Punishment

1985 Council of Europe Recommendations

1985 Declaration of Basic Principles of Justice for Victims of Crime and Abuse of Power

1989 Convention on the Rights of the Child

2000 Basic Principles and Guidelines on the Right to a Remedy and Reparation for Victims of Violations of International Human Rights and Humanitarian Law

Agreement between the United Nations and the Lebanese Republic on the establishment of a Special Tribunal for Lebanon annex to the Security Council Resolution 1757 of 30 May 2007

Agreement between the United Nations and the Royal Government of Cambodia concerning the prosecution under Cambodian law of crimes committed during the period of Democratic Kampuchea.

Hammurabi's Code of Laws

Manu's Code of Laws

Rule of Procedure and Evidence of the Special Tribunal for Lebanon

Statute of the Special Tribunal for Lebanon attached to the Security Council Resolution 1757 of 30 May 2007

The Charter of the International Military Tribunal for the Far East

The ICC Elements of Crimes

The ICC Regulations of the Trust Fund for Victims

The ICC Rules of Procedure and Evidence

The ICC Statute

The ICTR Rules of procedure and Evidence

The ICTR Rules of Procedure and Evidence

The ICTR Statute

The ICTY Statute

The Nuremberg International Military Tribunal Statute

SELECTED LEGAL TEXTS RELEVANT TO THE CONCEPT OF VICTIMS WITHIN THE ICC FRAMEWORK

The Rome Statute

Art 15(3)

If the Prosecutor concludes that there is a reasonable basis to proceed with an investigation, he or she shall submit to the Pre-Trial Chamber a request for authorization of an investigation, together with any supporting material collected. Victims may make representations to the Pre-Trial Chamber, in accordance with the Rules of Procedure and Evidence.

Art 19(3)

The Prosecutor may seek a ruling from the Court regarding a question of jurisdiction or admissibility. In proceedings with respect to jurisdiction or admissibility, those who have referred the situation under article 13, as well as victims, may also submit observations to the Court.

Art 43 (6)

The Registrar shall set up a Victims and Witnesses Unit within the Registry. This Unit shall provide, in consultation with the Office of the Prosecutor, protective measures and security arrangements, counseling and other appropriate assistance for witnesses, victims who appear before the Court, and others who are at risk on account of testimony given by such witnesses.

The Unit shall include staff with expertise in trauma, including trauma related to crimes of sexual violence.

Art 53

1. The Prosecutor shall, having evaluated the information made available to him or her, initiate an investigation unless he or she determines that there is no reasonable basis to proceed under this Statute. In deciding whether to initiate an investigation, the Prosecutor shall consider whether:

(a) The information available to the Prosecutor provides a reasonable basis to believe that a crime within the jurisdiction of the Court has been or is being committed;
(b) The case is or would be admissible under article 17; and
(c) Taking into account the gravity of the crime and the interests of victims, there are nonetheless substantial reasons to believe that an investigation would not serve the interests of justice. If the Prosecutor determines that there is no reasonable basis to proceed and his or her determination is based solely on subparagraph (c) above, he or she shall inform the Pre-Trial Chamber.

2. If, upon investigation, the Prosecutor concludes that there is not a sufficient basis for a prosecution because:

(a) There is not a sufficient legal or factual basis to seek a warrant or summons under article 58;
(b) The case is inadmissible under article 17; or
(c) A prosecution is not in the interests of justice, taking into account all the circumstances, including the gravity of the crime, the interests of victims and the age or infirmity of the alleged perpetrator, and his or her role in the alleged crime; the Prosecutor shall inform the Pre-Trial Chamber and the State making a referral under article 14 or the Security Council in a case under article 13, paragraph (b), of his or her conclusion and the reasons for the conclusion.

Art 54

1. The Prosecutor shall:

(a) In order to establish the truth, extend the investigation to cover all facts and evidence relevant to an assessment of whether there is criminal responsibility under this Statute, and, in doing so, investigate incriminating and exonerating circumstances equally;
(b) Take appropriate measures to ensure the effective investigation and prosecution of crimes within the jurisdiction of the Court, and in doing so, respect the interests and personal circumstances of victims and witnesses, including age, gender as defined in article 7, paragraph 3, and health, and take into account the nature of the crime, in particular where it involves sexual violence, gender violence or violence against children; and
(c) Fully respect the rights of persons arising under this Statute.

2. The Prosecutor may conduct investigations on the territory of a State:

(a) In accordance with the provisions of Part 9; or
(b) As authorized by the Pre-Trial Chamber under article 57, paragraph 3 (d).

3. The Prosecutor may:

(a) Collect and examine evidence;
(b) Request the presence of and question persons being investigated, victims and witnesses;
(c) Seek the cooperation of any State or intergovernmental organization or arrangement in accordance with its respective competence and/or mandate;
(d) Enter into such arrangements or agreements, not inconsistent with this Statute, as may be necessary to facilitate the cooperation of a State, intergovernmental organization or person;

(e) Agree not to disclose, at any stage of the proceedings, documents or information that the Prosecutor obtains on the condition of confidentiality and solely for the purpose of generating new evidence, unless the provider of the information consents; and
(f) Take necessary measures, or request that necessary measures be taken, to ensure the confidentiality of information, the protection of any person or the preservation of evidence.

Art 57 (3)

In addition to its other functions under this Statute, the Pre-Trial Chamber may:

(a) At the request of the Prosecutor, issue such orders and warrants as may be required for the purposes of an investigation;
(b) Upon the request of a person who has been arrested or has appeared pursuant to a summons under article 58, issue such orders, including measures such as those described in article 56, or seek such cooperation pursuant to Part 9 as may be necessary to assist the person in the preparation of his or her defence;
(c) Where necessary, provide for the protection and privacy of victims and witnesses, the preservation of evidence, the protection of persons who have been arrested or appeared in response to a summons, and the protection of national security information;
(d) Authorize the Prosecutor to take specific investigative steps within the territory of a State Party without having secured the cooperation of that State under Part 9 if, whenever possible having regard to the views of the State concerned, the Pre-Trial Chamber has determined in that case that the State is clearly unable to execute a request for cooperation due to the unavailability of any authority or any component of its judicial system competent to execute the request for cooperation under Part 9;
(e) Where a warrant of arrest or a summons has been issued under article 58, and having due regard to the strength of the evidence and the rights of the parties concerned, as provided for in this

Statute and the Rules of Procedure and Evidence, seek the cooperation of States pursuant to article 93, paragraph 1 (k), to take protective measures for the purpose of forfeiture, in particular for the ultimate benefit of victims.

Art 64 (2)

The Trial Chamber shall ensure that a trial is fair and expeditious and is conducted with full respect for the rights of the accused and due regard for the protection of victims and witnesses.

Art 64 (6)

In performing its functions prior to trial or during the course of a trial, the Trial Chamber may, as necessary:

(a) Exercise any functions of the Pre-Trial Chamber referred to in article 61, paragraph 11;
(b) Require the attendance and testimony of witnesses and production of documents and other evidence by obtaining, if necessary, the assistance of States as provided in this Statute;
(c) Provide for the protection of confidential information;
(d) Order the production of evidence in addition to that already collected prior to the trial or presented during the trial by the parties;
(e) Provide for the protection of the accused, witnesses and victims; and
(f) Rule on any other relevant matters.

Art 65 (4)

Where the Trial Chamber is of the opinion that a more complete presentation of the facts of the case is required in the interests of justice, in particular the interests of the victims, the Trial Chamber may:

(a) Request the Prosecutor to present additional evidence, including the testimony of witnesses; or
(b) Order that the trial be continued under the ordinary trial procedures provided by this Statute, in which case it shall consider the admission of guilt as not having been made and may remit the case to another Trial Chamber.

Art 68

1. The Court shall take appropriate measures to protect the safety, physical and psychological well-being, dignity and privacy of victims and witnesses. In so doing, the Court shall have regard to all relevant factors, including age, gender as defined in article 7, paragraph 3, and health, and the nature of the crime, in particular, but not limited to, where the crime involves sexual or gender violence or violence against children. The Prosecutor shall take such measures particularly during the investigation and prosecution of such crimes. These measures shall not be prejudicial to or inconsistent with the rights of the accused and a fair and impartial trial.
2. As an exception to the principle of public hearings provided for in article 67, the Chambers of the Court may, to protect victims and witnesses or an accused, conduct any part of the proceedings in camera or allow the presentation of evidence by electronic or other special means. In particular, such measures shall be implemented in the case of a victim of sexual violence or a child who is a victim or a witness, unless otherwise ordered by the Court, having regard to all the circumstances, particularly the views of the victim or witness.
3. Where the personal interests of the victims are affected, the Court shall permit their views and concerns to be presented and considered at stages of the proceedings determined to be appropriate by the Court and in a manner which is not prejudicial to or inconsistent with the rights of the accused and a fair and impartial trial. Such views and concerns may be presented by the legal representatives of

the victims where the Court considers it appropriate, in accordance with the Rules of Procedure and Evidence.

4. The Victims and Witnesses Unit may advise the Prosecutor and the Court on appropriate protective measures, security arrangements, counseling and assistance as referred to in article 43, paragraph 6.

Art 75

1. The Court shall establish principles relating to reparations to, or in respect of, victims, including restitution, compensation and rehabilitation. On this basis, in its decision the Court may, either upon request or on its own motion in exceptional circumstances, determine the scope and extent of any damage, loss and injury to, or in respect of, victims and will state the principles on which it is acting.
2. The Court may make an order directly against a convicted person specifying appropriate reparations to, or in respect of, victims, including restitution, compensation and rehabilitation. Where appropriate, the Court may order that the award for reparations be made through the Trust Fund provided for in article 79.
3. Before making an order under this article, the Court may invite and shall take account of representations from or on behalf of the convicted person, victims, other interested persons or interested States.
4. In exercising its power under this article, the Court may, after a person is convicted of a crime within the jurisdiction of the Court, determine whether, in order to give effect to an order which it may make under this article, it is necessary to seek measures under article 93, paragraph 1.
5. A State Party shall give effect to a decision under this article as if the provisions of article 109 were applicable to this article.
6. Nothing in this article shall be interpreted as prejudicing the rights of victims under national or international law.

Art 79 (1)

A Trust Fund shall be established by decision of the Assembly of States Parties for the benefit of victims of crimes within the jurisdiction of the Court, and of the families of such victims.

Art 82 (4)

A legal representative of the victims, the convicted person or a bona fide owner of property adversely affected by an order under article 75 may appeal against the order for reparations, as provided in the Rules of Procedure and Evidence.

Art 85 (1)

Anyone who has been the victim of unlawful arrest or detention shall have an enforceable right to compensation.

Art 87 (4)

In relation to any request for assistance presented under this Part, the Court may take such measures, including measures related to the protection of information, as may be necessary to ensure the safety or physical or psychological well-being of any victims, potential witnesses and their families. The Court may request that any information that is made available under this Part shall be provided and handled in a manner that protects the safety and physical or psychological well-being of any victims, potential witnesses and their families.

Art 90 (6)

In cases where paragraph 4 applies except that the requested State is under an existing international obligation to extradite the person to the requesting

State not Party to this Statute, the requested State shall determine whether to surrender the person to the Court or extradite the person to the requesting State.

In making its decision, the requested State shall consider all the relevant factors, including but not limited to:

(a) The respective dates of the requests;
(b) The interests of the requesting State including, where relevant, whether the crime was committed in its territory and the nationality of the victims and of the person sought; and
(c) The possibility of subsequent surrender between the Court and the requesting State.

Art 110 (4)

In its review under paragraph 3, the Court may reduce the sentence if it finds that one or more of the following factors are present:

(a) The early and continuing willingness of the person to cooperate with the Court in its investigations and prosecutions;
(b) The voluntary assistance of the person in enabling the enforcement of the judgments and orders of the Court in other cases, and in particular providing assistance in locating assets subject to orders of fine, forfeiture or reparation which may be used for the benefit of victims; or
(c) Other factors establishing a clear and significant change of circumstances

The Rules of Procedure and Evidence

Rule 16

1. In relation to victims, the Registrar shall be responsible for the performance of the following functions in accordance with the Statute and these Rules:

(a) Providing notice or notification to victims or their legal representatives;
(b) Assisting them in obtaining legal advice and organizing their legal representation, and providing their legal representatives with adequate support, assistance and information, including such facilities as may be necessary for the direct performance of their duty, for the purpose of protecting their rights during all stages of the proceedings in accordance with rules 89 to 91;
(c) Assisting them in participating in the different phases of the proceedings in accordance with rules 89 to 91;
(d) Taking gender-sensitive measures to facilitate the participation of victims of sexual violence at all stages of the proceedings.

2. In relation to victims, witnesses and others who are at risk on account of testimony given by such witnesses, the Registrar shall be responsible for the performance of the following functions in accordance with the Statute and these Rules:

(a) Informing them of their rights under the Statute and the Rules, and of the existence, functions and availability of the Victims and Witnesses Unit;
(b) Ensuring that they are aware, in a timely manner, of the relevant decisions of the Court that may have an impact on their interests, subject to provisions on confidentiality.

3. For the fulfillment of his or her functions, the Registrar may keep a special register for victims who have expressed their intention to participate in relation to a specific case.

4. Agreements on relocation and provision of support services on the territory of a State of traumatized or threatened victims, witnesses and others who are at risk on account of testimony given by such witnesses may be negotiated with the States by the Registrar on behalf of the Court. Such agreements may remain confidential.

Rule 17

1. The Victims and Witnesses Unit shall exercise its functions in accordance with article 43, paragraph 6.

2. The Victims and Witnesses Unit shall, *inter alia*, perform the following functions, in accordance with the Statute and the Rules, and in consultation with the Chamber, the Prosecutor and the defense, as appropriate:

(a) With respect to all witnesses, victims who appear before the Court, and others who are at risk on account of testimony given by such witnesses, in accordance with their particular needs and circumstances:

(i) Providing them with adequate protective and security measures and formulating long- and short-term plans for their protection;
(ii) Recommending to the organs of the Court the adoption of protection measures and also advising relevant States of such measures;
(iii) Assisting them in obtaining medical, psychological and other appropriate assistance;
(iv) Making available to the Court and the parties training in issues of trauma, sexual violence, security and confidentiality;
(v) Recommending, in consultation with the Office of the Prosecutor, the elaboration of a code of conduct, emphasizing the vital nature of security and confidentiality for investigators of the Court and of the defense and all intergovernmental and non-governmental organizations acting at the request of the Court, as appropriate;
(vi) Cooperating with States, where necessary, in providing any of the measures stipulated in this rule;

(b) With respect to witnesses:

(i) Advising them where to obtain legal advice for the purpose of protecting their rights, in particular in relation to their testimony;
(ii) Assisting them when they are called to testify before the Court;
(iii) Taking gender-sensitive measures to facilitate the testimony of victims of sexual violence at all stages of the proceedings.

3. In performing its functions, the Unit shall give due regard to the particular needs of children, elderly persons and persons with disabilities. In

order to facilitate the participation and protection of children as witnesses, the Unit may assign, as appropriate, and with the agreement of the parents or the legal guardian, a child-support person to assist a child through all stages of the proceedings.

Rule 18

For the efficient and effective performance of its work, the Victims and Witnesses Unit shall:

(a) Ensure that the staff in the Unit maintain confidentiality at all times;
(b) While recognizing the specific interests of the Office of the Prosecutor, the defense and the witnesses, respect the interests of the witness, including, where necessary, by maintaining an appropriate separation of the services provided to the prosecution and defense witnesses, and act impartially when cooperating with all parties and in accordance with the rulings and decisions of the Chambers;
(c) Have administrative and technical assistance available for witnesses, victims who appear before the Court, and others who are at risk on account of testimony given by such witnesses, during all stages of the proceedings and thereafter, as reasonably appropriate;
(d) Ensure training of its staff with respect to victims' and witnesses' security, integrity and dignity, including matters related to gender and cultural sensitivity;
(e) Where appropriate, cooperate with intergovernmental and non-governmental organizations.

Rule 40

1. For the purposes of article 50, paragraph 1, the following decisions shall be considered as resolving fundamental issues:

(a) All decisions of the Appeals Division;

(b) All decisions of the Court on its jurisdiction or on the admissibility of a case pursuant to articles 17, 18, 19 and 20;
(c) All decisions of a Trial Chamber on guilt or innocence, sentencing and reparations to victims pursuant to articles 74, 75 and 76;
(d) All decisions of a Pre-Trial Chamber pursuant to article 57, paragraph 3 (d).

Rule 43

The Court shall ensure that all documents subject to publication in accordance with the Statute and the Rules respect the duty to protect the confidentiality of the proceedings and the security of victims and witnesses.

Rule 50

1. When the Prosecutor intends to seek authorization from the Pre-Trial Chamber to initiate an investigation pursuant to article 15, paragraph 3, the Prosecutor shall inform victims, known to him or her or to the Victims and Witnesses Unit, or their legal representatives, unless the Prosecutor decides that doing so would pose a danger to the integrity of the investigation or the life or well-being of victims and witnesses. The Prosecutor may also give notice by general means in order to reach groups of victims if he or she determines in the particular circumstances of the case that such notice could not pose a danger to the integrity and effective conduct of the investigation or to the security and well-being of victims and witnesses. In performing these functions, the Prosecutor may seek the assistance of the Victims and Witnesses Unit as appropriate.
3. Following information given in accordance with sub-rule 1, victims may make representations in writing to the Pre-Trial Chamber within such time limit as set forth in the Regulations.
4. The Pre-Trial Chamber, in deciding on the procedure to be followed, may request additional information from the Prosecutor and from any of the victims who have made

representations, and, if it considers it appropriate, may hold a hearing.

5. The Pre-Trial Chamber shall issue its decision, including its reasons, as to whether to authorize the commencement of the investigation in accordance with article 15, paragraph 4, with respect to all or any part of the request by the Prosecutor. The Chamber shall give notice of the decision to victims who have made representations.

Rule 59(1)

For the purpose of article 19, paragraph 3, the Registrar shall inform the following of any question or challenge of jurisdiction or admissibility which has arisen pursuant to article 19, paragraphs 1, 2 and 3:

(a) Those who have referred a situation pursuant to article 13;
(b) The victims who have already communicated with the Court in relation to that case or their legal representatives.

Rule 70

In cases of sexual violence, the Court shall be guided by and, where appropriate, apply the following principles:

(a) Consent cannot be inferred by reason of any words or conduct of a victim where force, threat of force, coercion or taking advantage of a coercive environment undermined the victim's ability to give voluntary and genuine consent;
(b) Consent cannot be inferred by reason of any words or conduct of a victim where the victim is incapable of giving genuine consent;
(c) Consent cannot be inferred by reason of the silence of, or lack of resistance by, a victim to the alleged sexual violence;
(d) Credibility, character or predisposition to sexual availability of a victim or witness cannot be inferred by reason of the sexual nature of the prior or subsequent conduct of a victim or witness.

Rule 71

In the light of the definition and nature of the crimes within the jurisdiction of the Court, and subject to article 69, paragraph 4, a Chamber shall not admit evidence of the prior or subsequent sexual conduct of a victim or witness.

Rule 73 (3)

In making a decision under sub-rule 2, the Court shall give particular regard to recognizing as privileged those communications made in the context of the professional relationship between a person and his or her medical doctor, psychiatrist, psychologist or counselor, in particular those related to or involving victims, or between a person and a member of a religious clergy; and in the latter case, the Court shall recognize as privileged those communications made in the context of a sacred confession where it is an integral part of the practice of that religion.

Rule 71

In the light of the definition and nature of the crimes within the jurisdiction of the Court, and subject to article 69, paragraph 4, a Chamber shall not admit evidence of the prior or subsequent sexual conduct of a victim or witness.

Rule 72

1. Where there is an intention to introduce or elicit, including by means of the questioning of a victim or witness, evidence that the victim consented to an alleged crime of sexual violence, or evidence of the words, conduct, silence or lack of resistance of a victim or witness as referred to in principles (a) through (d) of rule 70, notification shall be provided to the Court which shall describe the substance of the evidence intended to be introduced or elicited and the relevance of the evidence to the issues in the case.

2. In deciding whether the evidence referred to in sub-rule 1 is relevant or admissible, a Chamber shall hear *in camera* the views of the Prosecutor, the defense, the witness and the victim or his or her legal representative, if any, and shall take into account whether that evidence has a sufficient degree of probative value to an issue in the case and the prejudice that such evidence may cause, in accordance with article 69, paragraph 4. For this purpose, the Chamber shall have regard to article 21, paragraph 3, and articles 67 and 68, and shall be guided by principles (a) to (d) of rule 70, especially with respect to the proposed questioning of a victim.

Rule 73

3. In making a decision under sub-rule 2, the Court shall give particular regard to recognizing as privileged those communications made in the context of the professional relationship between a person and his or her medical doctor, psychiatrist, psychologist or counselor, in particular those related to or involving victims, or between a person and a member of a religious clergy; and in the latter case, the Court shall recognize as privileged those communications made in the context of a sacred confession where it is an integral part of the practice of that religion.
6. If the Court determines that ICRC information, documents or other evidence are of great importance for a particular case, consultations shall be held between the Court and ICRC in order to seek to resolve the matter by cooperative means, bearing in mind the circumstances of the case, the relevance of the evidence sought, whether the evidence could be obtained from a source other than ICRC, the interests of justice and of victims, and the performance of the Court's and ICRC's functions.

Rule 76(4)

This rule is subject to the protection and privacy of victims and witnesses and the protection of confidential information as provided for in the Statute and rules 81 and 82.

Rule 81

3. Where steps have been taken to ensure the confidentiality of information, in accordance with articles 54, 57, 64, 72 and 93, and, in accordance with article 68, to protect the safety of witnesses and victims and members of their families, such information shall not be disclosed, except in accordance with those articles. When the disclosure of such information may create a risk to the safety of the witness, the Court shall take measures to inform the witness in advance.
4. The Chamber dealing with the matter shall, on its own motion or at the request of the Prosecutor, the accused or any State, take the necessary steps to ensure the confidentiality of information, in accordance with articles 54, 72 and 93, and, in accordance with article 68, to protect the safety of witnesses and victims and members of their families, including by authorizing the non-disclosure of their identity prior to the commencement of the trial.

Rule 85

For the purposes of the Statute and the Rules of Procedure and Evidence:

(a) "Victims" means natural persons who have suffered harm as a result of the commission of any crime within the jurisdiction of the Court;

(b) Victims may include organizations or institutions that have sustained direct harm to any of their property which is dedicated to religion, education, art or science or charitable purposes, and to their historic monuments, hospitals and other places and objects for humanitarian purposes.

Rule 86

A Chamber in making any direction or order, and other organs of the Court in performing their functions under the Statute or the Rules, shall take into account the needs of all victims and witnesses in accordance with article 68, in particular, children, elderly persons, persons with disabilities and victims of sexual or gender violence.

Rule 88

1. Upon the motion of the Prosecutor or the defense, or upon the request of a witness or a victim or his or her legal representative, if any, or on its own motion, and after having consulted with the Victims and Witnesses Unit, as appropriate, a Chamber may, taking into account the views of the victim or witness, order special measures such as, but not limited to, measures to facilitate the testimony of a traumatized victim or witness, a child, an elderly person or a victim of sexual violence, pursuant to article 68, paragraphs 1 and 2. The Chamber shall seek to obtain, whenever possible, the consent of the person in respect of whom the special measure is sought prior to ordering that measure.
2. A Chamber may hold a hearing on a motion or a request under sub-rule 1, if necessary *in camera* or *ex parte*, to determine whether to order any such special measure, including but not limited to an order that a counsel, a legal representative, a psychologist or a family member be permitted to attend during the testimony of the victim or the witness.
5. Taking into consideration that violations of the privacy of a witness or victim may create risk to his or her security, a Chamber shall be vigilant in controlling the manner of questioning a witness or victim so as to avoid any harassment or intimidation, paying particular attention to attacks on victims of crimes of sexual violence.

Rule 89

1. In order to present their views and concerns, victims shall make written application to the Registrar, who shall transmit the application to the relevant Chamber. Subject to the provisions of the Statute, in particular article 68, paragraph 1, the Registrar

shall provide a copy of the application to the Prosecutor and the defense, who shall be entitled to reply within a time limit to be set by the Chamber. Subject to the provisions of sub-rule 2, the Chamber shall then specify the proceedings and manner in which participation is considered appropriate, which may include making opening and closing statements.

2. The Chamber, on its own initiative or on the application of the Prosecutor or the defense, may reject the application if it considers that the person is not a victim or that the criteria set forth in article 68, paragraph 3, are not otherwise fulfilled. A victim whose application has been rejected may file a new application later in the proceedings.
3. An application referred to in this rule may also be made by a person acting with the consent of the victim, or a person acting on behalf of a victim, in the case of a victim who is a child or, when necessary, a victim who is disabled.

Rule 90

1. A victim shall be free to choose a legal representative.
2. Where there are a number of victims, the Chamber may, for the purposes of ensuring the effectiveness of the proceedings, request the victims or particular groups of victims, if necessary with the assistance of the Registry, to choose a common legal representative or representatives. In facilitating the coordination of victim representation, the Registry may provide assistance, *inter alia*, by referring the victims to a list of counsel, maintained by the Registry, or suggesting one or more common legal representatives.
3. If the victims are unable to choose a common legal representative or representatives within a time limit that the Chamber may decide, the Chamber may request the Registrar to choose one or more common legal representatives.
4. The Chamber and the Registry shall take all reasonable steps to ensure that in the selection of common legal representatives, the distinct interests of the victims, particularly as provided in article 68, paragraph 1, are represented and that any conflict of interest is avoided.

5. A victim or group of victims who lack the necessary means to pay for a common legal representative chosen by the Court may receive assistance from the Registry, including, as appropriate, financial assistance.
6. A legal representative of a victim or victims shall have the qualifications set forth in rule 22, sub-rule 1.

Rule 91 (2)

2. A legal representative of a victim shall be entitled to attend and participate in the proceedings in accordance with the terms of the ruling of the Chamber and any modification thereof given under rules 89 and 90. This shall include participation in hearings unless, in the circumstances of the case, the Chamber concerned is of the view that the representative's intervention should be confined to written observations or submissions. The Prosecutor and the defense shall be allowed to reply to any oral or written observation by the legal representative for victims.

Rule 92

1. This rule on notification to victims and their legal representatives shall apply to all proceedings before the Court, except in proceedings provided for in Part 2.

2. In order to allow victims to apply for participation in the proceedings in accordance with rule 89, the Court shall notify victims concerning the decision of the Prosecutor not to initiate an investigation or not to prosecute pursuant to article 53. Such a notification shall be given to victims or their legal representatives who have already participated in the proceedings or, as far as possible, to those who have communicated with the Court in respect of the situation or case in question. The Chamber may order the measures outlined in sub-rule 8 if it considers it appropriate in the particular circumstances.

3. In order to allow victims to apply for participation in the proceedings in accordance with rule 89, the Court shall notify victims regarding its decision to hold a hearing to confirm charges pursuant to article 61. Such a notification shall be given to victims or their legal representatives who have

already participated in the proceedings or, as far as possible, to those who have communicated with the Court in respect of the case in question.

4. When a notification for participation as provided for in sub-rules 2 and 3 has been given, any subsequent notification as referred to in sub-rules 5 and 6 shall only be provided to victims or their legal representatives who may participate in the proceedings in accordance with a ruling of the Chamber pursuant to rule 89 and any modification thereof.

5. In a manner consistent with the ruling made under rules 89 to 91, victims or their legal representatives participating in proceedings shall, in respect of those proceedings, be notified by the Registrar in a timely manner of:

(a) Proceedings before the Court, including the date of hearings and any postponements thereof, and the date of delivery of the decision;
(b) Requests, submissions, motions and other documents relating to such requests, submissions or motions.

6. Where victims or their legal representatives have participated in a certain stage of the proceedings, the Registrar shall notify them as soon as possible of the decisions of the Court in those proceedings.

Rule 93 Views of victims or their legal representatives

A Chamber may seek the views of victims or their legal representatives participating pursuant to rules 89 to 91 on any issue, *inter alia*, in relation to issues referred to in rules 107, 109, 125, 128, 136, 139 and 191. In addition, a Chamber may seek the views of other victims, as appropriate.

Rule 94 (1)

A victim's request for reparations under article 75 shall be made in writing and filed with the Registrar. It shall contain the following particulars:

(a) The identity and address of the claimant;
(b) A description of the injury, loss or harm;
(c) The location and date of the incident and, to the extent possible, the identity of the person or persons the victim believes to be responsible for the injury, loss or harm;

Rule 95

1. In cases where the Court intends to proceed on its own motion pursuant to article 75, paragraph 1, it shall ask the Registrar to provide notification of its intention to the person or persons against whom the Court is considering making a determination, and, to the extent possible, to victims, interested persons and interested States. Those notified shall file with the Registry any representation made under article 75, paragraph 3.

2. If, as a result of notification under sub-rule 1:

(a) A victim makes a request for reparations, that request will be determined as if it had been brought under rule 94;
(b) A victim requests that the Court does not make an order for reparations, the Court shall not proceed to make an individual order in respect of that victim.

Rule 96

1. Without prejudice to any other rules on notification of proceedings, the Registrar shall, insofar as practicable, notify the victims or their legal representatives and the person or persons concerned. The Registrar shall also, having regard to any information provided by the Prosecutor, take all the necessary measures to give adequate publicity of the reparation proceedings before the Court, to the extent possible, to other victims, interested persons and interested States.

Rule 97

2. At the request of victims or their legal representatives, or at the request of the convicted person, or on its own motion, the Court may appoint appropriate experts to assist it in determining the scope, extent of any damage, loss and injury to, or in respect of victims and to suggest various options concerning the appropriate types and modalities of reparations. The Court shall invite, as appropriate, victims or their legal representatives, the convicted person as well as interested persons and interested

States to make observations on the reports of the experts.

3. In all cases, the Court shall respect the rights of victims and the convicted person.

Rule 98 (2)

2. The Court may order that an award for reparations against a convicted person be deposited with the Trust Fund where at the time of making the order it is impossible or impracticable to make individual awards directly to each victim. The award for reparations thus deposited in the Trust Fund shall be separated from other resources of the Trust Fund and shall be forwarded to each victim as soon as possible.

Rule 119 (1)

Before imposing or amending any conditions restricting liberty, the Pre-Trial Chamber shall seek the views of the Prosecutor, the person concerned, any relevant State and victims that have communicated with the Court in that case and whom the Chamber considers could be at risk as a result of a release or conditions imposed.

Rule 121 (10)

The Registry shall create and maintain a full and accurate record of all proceedings before the Pre-Trial Chamber, including all documents transmitted to the Chamber pursuant to this rule. Subject to any restrictions concerning confidentiality and the protection of national security information, the record may be consulted by the Prosecutor, the person and victims or their legal representatives participating in the proceedings pursuant to rules 89 to 91.

Rule 131 (1)

Subject to any restrictions concerning confidentiality and the protection of national security information, the record may be consulted by the Prosecutor, the defense, the representatives of States when they participate in the proceedings, and the victims or their legal representatives participating in the proceedings pursuant to rules 89 to 91.

Rule 143

Pursuant to article 76, paragraphs 2 and 3, for the purpose of holding a further hearing on matters related to sentence and, if applicable, reparations, the Presiding Judge shall set the date of the further hearing. This hearing can be postponed, in exceptional circumstances, by the Trial Chamber, on its own motion or at the request of the Prosecutor, the defense or the legal representatives of the victims participating in the proceedings pursuant to rules 89 to 91 and, in respect of reparations hearings, those victims who have made a request under rule 94.

Rule 144

Decisions of the Trial Chamber concerning admissibility of a case, the jurisdiction of the Court, criminal responsibility of the accused, sentence and reparations shall be pronounced in public and, wherever possible, in the presence of the accused, the Prosecutor, the victims or the legal representatives of the victims participating in the proceedings pursuant to rules 89 to 91, and the representatives of the States which have participated in the proceedings.

Rule 194 (1)

If protective measures within the meaning of article 68 have been adopted, the Prosecutor or Chamber, as appropriate, shall consider the views of the Chamber which ordered the measures as well as those of the relevant victim or witness, before deciding on the request.

Rule 221

1. The Presidency shall, after having consulted, as appropriate, with the Prosecutor, the sentenced person, the victims or their legal representatives, the national authorities of the State of enforcement or any relevant third party,

or representatives of the Trust Fund provided for in article 79, decide on all matters related to the disposition or allocation of property or assets realized through enforcement of an order of the Court.

2. In all cases, when the Presidency decides on the disposition or allocation of property or assets belonging to the sentenced person, it shall give priority to the enforcement of measures concerning reparations to victims.